COMMEDIA IN PERFORMANCE

THE THREE CUCKOLDS

by Leon Katz

Based on an anonymous commedia dell' arte scenario

THEATRE BOOK PUBLISHERS
211 West 71 St. New York, N.Y. 10023

Copyright © 1958, 1986 by Leon Katz. All rights reserved.

CAUTION: Professionals and amateurs are hereby warned that *The Three Cuckolds,* being fully protected under the Copyright Laws of the United States of America, the British Commonwealth, including the Dominion of Canada, and all other countries of the International Copyright Union and the Universal Copyright Convention, is subject to royalty. All rights, including professional, amateur, motion picture, recitation, lecturing, public reading, radio and television broadcasting, and the rights of translation into foreign languages, are strictly reserved. Particular emphasis is laid on the question of readings, permission for which must be secured in writing from the author's agent.

All inquiries concerning rights for *The Three Cuckolds* are addressed exclusively to Samuel French, Inc., 25 West 45th Street, New York, NY, 10036, without whose permission in writing no use of the play may be made.

Library of Congress Cataloging-in-Publication Data

Katz, Leon, 1919–
 The three cuckolds.

 "Based on an anonymous commedia dell' arte scenario."
  1. Commédia dell'arte. I. Title.
PS3561.A76T47 1986   812'.54   86-22302
ISBN 0-936839-06-6

APPLAUSE THEATRE BOOK PUBLISHERS
211 W. 71st St. New York, NY 10023
(212) 595-4735

All rights reserved. Printed in the U.S.A.

First Applause Printing, 1986

PREFACE

(Biancolelli, having finished reading the text of The Three Cuckolds, *tosses it off his lap and looks glum.)*

BIANCOLELLI. It's positively sinful writing down all the words of a commedia farce. The life of commedia dell' arte was in actors, not in writers; not in what was memorized and rehearsed, but in their spur-of-the-moment invention.

LK. That is typical actor's myopia. You were commedia's great Arlecchino, yes, but you were also the friend and mentor of Moliere. Do you suppose that the words of his comedies and farces should have been left for his actors to invent?

BIANCOLELLI. Moliere's is a very different art from commedia's. To confuse one with the other does no service to either. The genius, the glory of commedia was in us, the actors—our imagination, our agility, our words. The magic of the art was in us, in our bodies, with which we performed wonders.

LK. But the stories of those wonders strain belief. How could they be true? The story of the zany, for example, who astounded spectators in the Venetian piazza with over a hundred variations of a single somersault. Impossible. And that other Arlecchino who is supposed to have done his dances and acrobatics right up to his death at the age of ninety. Ridiculous stories, characteristic of the nonsense written about the actors' skills.

BIANCOLELLI. Why impossible? You who were never there, can you question our daring and our skill?

LK. I can not. But what I do question, what I can't get straight through all the mists of myth, is precisely what that skill was, exactly what the art of commedia was, and what the difference is between the reality and the myth.

BIANCOLELLI. I cannot tell you because I do not know the myth. I can tell you what I remember, and that's astonishing enough.

LK. Very well, let me hear it from your own mouth.

BIANCOLELLI. This is how it was. Extraordinary actors with extraordinary genius assembled like a family and performed together for years, each actor developing his role—his 'mask'—over a lifetime. Their children after them inherited the traditions of their elders and built on them from generation to generation. When we performed, we would glance at a scenario off-stage, make note of the gist of the scene we were about to play, and improvise on the spot our business and our dialogue on the basis of nothing but the scenario's slender hints. And each of us, since we were committed to our mask for a lifetime, developed our role as what you would call now a 'star turn,' but still in marvelously harmonious relation to the ensemble. We could do any number of remarkable things—acrobatic stunts, dancing, improvised dialogue—but the essence, the very essence of our performing was in our ability to express ourselves—so to speak, talk—with and through our bodies. Why? Because we wore masks, and with that fixed expression covering our faces, expressivity had to come from an infinitely supple vocabulary developed by the whole body. That is how it was.

LK. I don't believe a word of it.

PREFACE

BIANCOLELLI. How can you dare to disbelieve? That is the whole truth.

LK. It's hardly a corner of it. I had supposed that the myth grew only over the last three hundred years, but I find it in your seventeenth-century mouth as well. It's an inviting myth, to be sure, positively astonishing, but it strains my sense of the limits of human capacity. I've read the scenarios, I've even plagiarized from them, and know that some of their scenes are marvelously, hideously complex. They depend on precise timing of action and precise balance and pointing of dialogue. Actors capable of improvising such dialogue and action on the basis of a glance at a scenario couldn't have been human but literally divine.

BIANCOLELLL We were.

LK. I can hardly grant that. I grant only that your ability to express yourselves through your bodies was awfully good, but all the exaggerations of your prowess, and the conventions and frozen stylizations of movement associated with your acting come mostly from illustrations of commedia done in and since your century. They then, like you now, did much to create the fiction. Do you know Jacques Callot, the great seventeenth-century artist? To my mind, he did commedia the greatest service and the greatest disservice of any of the long line of commedia image-makers.

BIANCOLELLI. The Balli di Sfessania engravings.

LK. Those. In that series he shows commedia performers on the trestle stages they used in street performances. And what are the actors doing? Callot shows them in contortion, dancing, whirling, almost flying, all wearing much the same kind of mask and much the same kind of costume with phallic emblems or shadowy outlines of them in their breeches, strumming on instruments that may or may not ever have existed, and moving like balletic whirlwinds. Is this conceivably the reality of commedia performance? No. It may have been Callot's fantasy of the spirit, the idea of commedia—the spirit of its movement, its vulgarity, its noisy hilarity. But the actors were rarely clothed as he clothed them, were rarely so balletic in their movement.

BIANCOLELLL Your skepticism is based on your own fancies, and my guess is that you the writer are determined to make as little as possible of the role of us, the actors.

LK. There are records—apart from fanciful illustrations like Callot's—and they support the belief that the greatest actors, those famous throughout Europe, were, to be sure, equal to remarkable feats of skill and grace of movement. But they also corroborate the suspicion that the others, much like contemporary actors, were mostly middling talents or no good at all. Nor can the obstacle of the masks justify the belief that the companies were families of acrobatic mimes and whirling dervishes. Only four of the standard characters—Pantalone, Dottore, Capitano and the zany (your Arlecchino and his variants)—wore masks at all. The rest of the company was unmasked and had no need of all that 'expressive' bodily contortion. And so the impression of commedia actors adopting a special mode of stylized, mime-like performance is also an over-elaborated, idealized extension of the fact—in other words, a myth.

BIANCOLELLI. I begin to wonder which myth is the greater—Callot's or yours.

LK. His, certainly. What is the reality? More ordinary, I'm sure, but certainly more believable.

BIANCOLELLI. And you, I suppose, know this reality.

LK. I know at least this much of it. First, the companies didn't start the tradition. Early in the sixteenth century, before there were any, there were solo performers hired by merchants on market-days to attract crowds with their singing, dancing, tumbling and tricks. When the crowd was large enough, the merchant would push the clown aside and sell his wares. The performers were called zanni—as they gained reputation, they adopted professional names such as Zan Polo, Zan Fritada, Zan Farina, as if to say, delectable to eat. Now if Callot was illustrating anything remotely connected with reality, it was these street zanies in their crude skits tricked out with songs and dances, cribbing from medieval farce— the conventional quarrel scene, for example, ending with the clubbing and drubbing of a Punch-and-Judy husband and wife.

BIANCOLELLI. Crude! Crude, you say! Where, tell me, is the crudity in comedians—in the street or on the stage— who can keep crowds laughing until their sides split, and who can awe them out of their minds with a hundred variations of your basic somersault?

LK. A hundred variations of—myth, myth!

BIANCOLELLI. Myth yourself! Was it a myth to that Englishman hurrying to the Doge's palace—we have his own letter, have you read it?—caught for two hours in the Piazza San Marco and unable to move one step because of the crowds of thousands filling every inch of the piazza mesmerized by one comedian improvising at a merchant's stall? Two hours—al fresco—and no one moved!

LK. If no one moved, it was not for the improvisations alone. They all had fixed and memorized poems, songs and dialogues, and improvised a bit around those, just like contemporary stand-up comics.

BIANCOLELLI. A bit!

LK. A bit, and perhaps a bit more, just as you did when the companies were finally formed out of these street professionals and some devoted amateurs. And we have the contract from one of these companies, so that we can glean from it exactly how—in reality—they were set up. Nine actors—by your time, ten or twelve was the usual number—a standard role assigned to each, as, Pantalone, Dottore, and so on, were hired by contract for only one year's service. If they left the company before year's end, they were heavily fined, but still actors did leave, not infrequently, for reasons that give us insight into the degree to which the companies functioned as real ensembles, and the degree to which each actor was bent on advancing his own career. Their sort of ensemble shows up thoroughly in the letters they wrote to their ducal patrons, filled with accounts of bitter quarrels that broke up companies, and that—

BIANCOLELLI. What in heaven's name have letters like that to do with ensemble acting? They quarrelled, yes, because there were jealousies among lovers and their mistresses, that sort of thing, but—

LK. There were fights brought on by professional jealousies, too. Do you remember the scenario called La Pazzia, The Madwoman, in which Isabella goes mad when she's rejected by her lover?

BIANCOLELLI. Who doesn't?

LK. Her mad scene featured a long soliloquy, the madwoman's tirade, the role's show-piece. Well, in one of the companies, two innamorati, the female lovers, a Flamina and a Vittoria, both treasured the role, and they fought so bitterly over it that the company split, each faction forming a new company. Later both companies scheduled performances of the play in the same city on the same day, and the battle lines were drawn. Spectators loyal to each actress joined in the feud, and the street brawls that followed had to be stopped by the constabulary. Now, we're familiar in our own time with similar manifestations of party loyalty—Maria Callas and Renata Tebaldi factions, for example, among opera buffs—but they're rarely moved to push their loyalties to the point of battling in the streets. Oh, no, commedia stars then were like opera stars now, only worse. They treasured—no, better, greedily harbored—their roles, as often as not at the expense of the ensemble.

BIANCOLELLI. Hopeless comparison! Your opera stars play many roles in a career, commedia actors only one. They adopted one mask to which they devoted a lifetime, developing it, transforming it, creating it anew. Of course we were jealous of our roles. They were ours; we owned them, they owned us, all our lives.

LK. Of all the fictions that attach to commedia dell'arte, that one, in the face of the facts, is the most bizarre.

BIANCOLELLI. Bizarre! You tell me, you who were never there, that it's fiction, bizarre, when I myself, I, I, was Arlecchino, Arlecchino and no one but Arlecchino, all my professional life!

LK. We have contracts, as I've said, and anyone can read in them how actors were hired to play not one role but as many as three in a single season.

BIANCOLELLI. And what sort of actors were those? Sodden amateurs, hired by impoverished companies crawling about the miserable countryside in broken-down carts, barely able to sustain a performance, let alone a mask for a lifetime.

LK. Not precisely. One of the greatest of all commedia actors, Francesco Andreini, began his career playing concurrently the masks of Pantalone, Zanni and the Magician. It was only later that he became famous in the role of the Lover, and, advanced in years, played Capitano until his retirement. And he was not alone. Other actors who became famous played several roles concurrently, and retiring from one mask to adopt another wasn't all that uncommon. You pretend to ignorance and shock at the very thought of commedia actors playing all over the lot, but you remember very well, I'm sure, how companies in Italy at the height of their fame would be invited to court at Paris, for example, but with the stipulation that the company, celebrated for its star players, come intact. But where would the star players be? As often as not, off with another company that season, which meant quick negotiation for substitutes from still other companies—in mid-season—to join the troupe at court. Your model, then, of a unified ensemble together for years, each of its members developing expertise in his own mask over the years, doesn't hold. In reality, actors then like actors now took different roles and joined different companies on year-to-year contracts, sometimes remaining for a stretch of years but, off contract, free to move wherever they pleased.

BIANCOLELLI. Your 'reality' takes the heart out of a beautiful art, and makes usual what wasn't at all usual, commonplace what was unique. What else of the memory of my beloved commedia are you determined to destroy?

LK. The part of the myth to which most homage has been paid, the one that most thoroughly distorts its realities: improvisation during performance.

BIANCOLELLI. *(Emits a bitter laugh, says nothing, but looks worried.)*

LK. Oh, yes, the actors did, I suppose, glance at a scenario off-stage to make certain of the action of the scene they were about to play. But were the scenarios nothing but casual memory hints? Far from it. They were carefully

PREFACE

constructed scene outlines prepared by the company's director (usually its leading actor), sometimes by the producer (a non-actor), and once in a great while by the company as a whole. But rarely was a scenario put together from new material thought up by the actors themselves. They were usually assembled from bits and pieces of familiar speeches, scenes and stories taken from other scenarios and from written plays, a mixture of standard tales and situations used in play after play. A good while before each performance, the company was instructed in a new scenario, and then each member went off for private preparation and study. Do you remember, Signor Biancolelli, this all-important phase of preparation? If you do, and admit to it, then you'll concede that my suspicions are justified as to how much improvisation was and was not practiced.

BIANCOLELLI. I admit nothing and concede nothing. May your suspicions die with you unless you have the strongest evidence—

LK. It couldn't be stronger, and you're the last man in the world who can afford to deny it. The evidence is yours.

BIANCOLELLI. Mine!

LK. Yours and others like you who had the generosity to publish—

BIANCOLELLI. Publish! What?

LK. Your private commonplace book in which were set down ready-made speeches, dialogues and complete scenes, all memorized and rehearsed. Domenico Biancolelli, the great Arlecchino, published all the memorized scenes in his repertory—memorized by himself and the other actors who played in his scenes, and they're all recorded for posterity. At a guess, I'd say that your written material took up about a third of the play's text and stage business. And if you add to this estimate the estimate of the memorized passages of the other actors in their scenes without Arlecchino, it's fairly obvious that the art of improvisation had less to do with inventing matter while performing than with merely playing variations on familiar and practiced material. Really, much the same procedure as stand-up comics follow today.

BIANCOLELLI. *(Outflanked, looking miserable, holds his peace.)*

LK. Still, really, where is the shame in that? The published texts give every evidence of the impossibility of anyone's rattling them off spontaneously in the midst of a performance. They depend for their effectiveness on a host of complicated rhetorical devices: rhymed tags at the ends of speeches, alternation of conceits, paired and contrasted, in lovers' dialogues, sustained apostrophes and antitheses in prose duets that sometimes run for pages. The precision, the complexity, the implied speed of delivery and the sheer quantity of these dialogues for a single play couldn't possibly be caught on the wing of the moment's inspiration. There's no shame in that, Signor Biancolelli. There's no reason to conceal the fact. And what was true of the dialogues was also true of the set soliloquies, wasn't it? Isabella's mad aria, for example, was made up of a scramble of surreal non-sequiturs, was written out (it's extant) and then elaborated, expanded, by different actresses. But for all the elaborations and additions through which it may have gone, it remained the standard pazzia scene, with a more or less fixed text, done again and again in much the same way.

BIANCOLELLI. You burrow through old histories and scratch through old texts, and think you've come up with the secret of commedia dell'arte. No, you say, it wasn't the actors, it was the scenarios and the written dialogues; it

PREFACE xv

wasn't improvisation, it was memory and rehearsal. Child, do you imagine you can catch the genius of an art by footnoting its lapses from its own ideal? Suppose the words we used *were* in our commonplace books? Do you know how they got there? Who put them there? *We* were the writers—

LK. The plagiarizers.

BIANCOLELLI. And you?

LK. True.

BIANCOLELLI. And from whom did we plagiarize—or rather borrow and make our own? Do you remember Isabella Andreini, the great Isabella, who is still thought even in your time to have been the greatest actress the western world has ever known? The great Isabella, great not only for her acting but for her learning and her writing, studied not only the classics but her own contemporaries. She was positively learned in Dante, Petrarch, Boccaccio—in all the great poets and philosophers—whom she incorporated into her own memorized dialogue. She was a learned and brilliant woman, so much so that she was invited to membership in the Academies. And there were other testimonials to her wonder. In Lyons where she died of a miscarriage on her way back from an engagement in Paris, she was honored with a municipal funeral, and several courts of Europe went into official mourning for a month. Learned, beautiful, virtuous—a not so uncommon thing among us actors—devoted to her husband Francesco whom she bore seven children, a great actress and a gifted writer, she was more than equal to the job of filling out with both her own and borrowed rhetoric the bare bones of the scenarios' innamorata scenes of 'scorned love,' 'reciprocal love,' 'disdainful love,' 'lovers' jealousy,' 'lovers' reconciliation,' and so on. You, footnote fiddler, don't you realize that you can't separate the commedia text from the commedia actor, whether he makes it up in the rush of the performance or sets it down in the leisure of his study? It is his, wholly his—the marvel of it—it all comes finally from him alone. There's no other art like it, never was nor will be, none.

LK. What I realize is simply that—

BIANCOLELLI. *(Now launched, and not to be interrupted)* And there was more we 'borrowed'—stole, you say, very well, stole. But not from poets and playwrights, no, from ourselves, from one another. The common coin of comedians, stores and stores of it accumulated over aeons and still stored now in your own time—the signature, the nub of commedia dell'arte. Your Chaplin, in his Gold Rush—do you remember?—dines with manner, with superb grace, on his boiled shoe. I say with pride: your Chaplin stole his dinner from Arlecchino. It was kind of him to pay us homage because, with genius, he kept alive commedia's lazzi, those interpolated bits of comic business done for the most part by characters like my own—the servants, the zanni. I'm about to go on stage; I glance at the scenario, and read: 'Pantalone leaves. Arlecchino enters and does the lazzo of the fly.' Memorized? Yes. Improvised? Yes. Both at once. After a hundred times before the crowd, the lazzo of the fly is in my memory, my mouth, my body, my bones. And yet now it will be done for the first time, as though it has never been done before. I come in holding my empty stomach, bemoaning my hunger; for days I've eaten nothing, not a radish, not a seed, nothing; and I moan hunger, hunger so great I'll eat anything, but what is there to—? A buzzing; I turn my head; here, there; I see a fly. Eyes narrow, I follow it, it settles; a stealthy approach, long, long, slow, slow— it's gone. Despair. A buzzing; eyes dart this way, that;

again I see it; follow it; it settles—on my nose! I am wood, stone; a finger moves, a hand, arm, slowly, like a heavy crane, the arm up, almost to the nose—the fly is gone! Mute, wild despair. Again the buzzing; I stalk; it flies high—I leap up (hunting dog); it flies low to the ground—I tense on all fours (a cat), stalk, stalk, stalk —I seize it! I sit on the ground, crosslegged, peek into cupped hands, great smile—my dinner! With aplomb, with manner, with superb grace, I eat my dainty, one wing, then another, then feet, then head, then body, in small bites, until the banquet is done. Then politely, like your Chaplin, a genteel burp.

Low? Outrageous? Yes. Outrageous comedy, provoking the lowest kind of laughter. Commedia shares with low comedy everywhere and in every time the lowest of comic motives: food, sex and money. All the comic masks in commedia pursue them, but the masks most driven by these urges are the zanni, and they pursue them with the holy zeal of great men pursuing noble office. But below this lowness, there is wisdom. Did you catch it, you who have crawled through all the texts and records? The note of wisdom exploited in this off-the-plot interruption, this lazzo of the fly, is the one your Chaplin also discovered working in the same low vein. When he was asked to define comedy, he did so in three words: 'Comedy is tragedy.' The more awful, the more devastating, the more thoroughly humiliating the situation is for the sadly comic character, the more hilarious he seems. And so the two most side-splitting situations in commedia lazzi are madness and suicide. You find that hard to believe? Then you'll find harder to believe what lies below *that* wisdom. Listen for it: the lazzo of suicide.

I, Arlecchino, have just heard Columbina finally and forever reject my love. In your ordinary play, your written play, what would your wise writer out of his largesse give this Arlecchino to do? Strapped within the jacket of the plot, 'Ungrateful woman!' I'd cry, 'Ah, I am in despair!' Brief lamentation, and then, 'What shall I do now? Try again to win her or be revenged?' Not so in commedia, because commedia accommodates a bit of a hiatus between 'I despair' and "What shall I do?' And into that gap, I, Arlecchino-Biancolelli, insert the real wisdom of commedia's lowest vein, in the lazzo of suicide, and in it touch on—no, wildly exaggerate—the human understanding, everyone's, of absolute loss. Of Columbina? Partly, only partly. Of self-esteem? Entirely. The more I, Arlecchino, already the lowest of creatures in the eyes of men, lose my self-esteem—the more bluntly I'm faced with my own nonentity—the more I want to settle for death. 'Only one thing for me to do,' I reason. 'Kill myself.' I proceed, with ineptitude, but with a certain Don Quixote-ish rationale. What will this suicide accomplish for me? Obviously, it will recover my self-esteem 'because,' I tell myself, 'it will be recorded in ancient and modern history.' The procedure is simple: I toss a rope over a cross-beam, kick away a chair, and the thing is done. Now the rope is around my neck—lamentation—I'm about to kick the chair when— wait! 'This, for Columbina? For a woman? And will it make me any fatter? No, it will make me hideously thinner.' I get off the chair. I argue with myself, back and forth, this way, that, jesuitical—and resolve again on hanging. Rope tight around my neck, about to kick the chair again—a new consideration: it's an ordinary death and so there's little honor in it. No, I must die an extraordinary death, an Arlecchinoesque death. Off the chair again, deliberating. But no way comes to me, none that will satisfy what I really crave from death: honor, self-esteem. I turn to the spectators. 'Gentle creatures, would one of you be good enough to die first,

PREFACE   xix

to show me how? I'll be very much obliged to you.' No one obliges. But I note: the spectators are laughing. Ah, I recollect, 'I've heard people say, I laughed until I nearly died.' A hope. I try, hard, but have little cause for laughter. An idea: tickling. I tickle myself; I laugh. I tickle more, I laugh, laugh, roll across the stage floor for minutes on end in convulsions trying to tickle myself to death until I'm interrupted by Pasquariello. Hiatus over, the plot is back.

Do you see?—You see nothing, right? Ah, you writer, with all your sleuthing and all your crying "myth, myth,' you'll never catch the secret of commedia's art. Because it's not *in* the scenarios, the illustrations, the letters, or even in the texts I was foolish enough to publish myself. It's here—and here—and here—and here.

(He touches his head, his heart, his stomach, and his behind.)

It's in the common wisdom of the victim, the underdog, the put-upon, who know all the hurts, and love to see their familiar aches and pains in wild, in magical colors. Now, my poor near-sighted friend, if you want to see commedia dell'arte live again in your century as it did so gloriously in mine—but do you?

LK. Yes, of course! Yes, yes!

BIANCOLELLI. Then bury your suspicions and your doubts about how commedia performances were made in my time —how much written, how much improvised? how much rehearsed, how much invented on the wing?—and know that all those myths of impossible feats of skill, of devoted ensembles, of dedication to a role for a lifetime and the rest of them are more real, closer to the facts, than are the facts. Believe me, those awesome myths of the prowess, greatness, genius of commedia dell'arte in my time might just conceivably inspire such prowess, greatness and genius in yours. In that hope and to that end, interr your sodden facts, hide them, let them remain our secret.

LK. To be sure, you are right. Very well—those facts shall remain our secret. I promise—no, I swear—I won't tell a soul.

New Haven, 1986

THE
THREE CUCKOLDS

An anonymous scenario of the commedia dell' arte
converted into a play by Leon Katz

CHARACTERS

(In order of their appearance)

ARLECCHINO

COVIELLO

FLAMINIA

PANTALONE

ZANNI

FRANCESCHINA

DEVIL

LEANDRO

CINTIA

MUSICIAN

SCENE: *A street before three houses*

ACT I

SCENE 1

ARLECCHINO *comes in calling to someone, it seems, off stage.*

ARLECCHINO. Arlecchino! Arlecchino! Look what we've found! Move, you scrawny little centipede! Oh, look at him move —like a couple of worms wrapping themselves around a stick! Hurry up, run, we've stumbled on the door of salvation! Oh you snail, can't you shove along any faster? We're only four steps, three hugs, two kisses and a how-are-you from a mountain of food and drink!

Then, as though he has just come in, bedraggled, exhausted, he answers himself.

Food and drink? Where? Zno food and drink. Just doors, houses. Kicks, bruises. No sleep, no meat, no wine, no——

He interrupts himself impatiently.

Doors and houses! Yes, but whose?

Not interested.

Whose?

Shouting at himself impatiently.

Cintia's! We've stumbled on Cintia's door!

His weariness disappearing.

Cintia, the kitchen queen?

Going to her door.

Oh, sweet promise, sweetest Cintia, remember when last we met? Remember the knock at the door? And remember how soon we parted? And what did you whisper to me when that husband, that snooper, that rheumy Coviello was burrowing through your cupboards and nosing through your pails? "A lover? A lover? A lover?" he shrieked. And, injured as you were, what was it you whispered to your poor Arlecchino hanging by a nail from your window? "Come back," you sighed, "come back and we'll be quits with the old fool for what he has made us bear."

He pretends to open wide an enormous pocket in his clothing.

Pocket, remember? Do you have it still? I begged you to hold tight to Cintia's promise.

He so-to-speak lifts it from his pocket and holds it up tenderly.

Sweet promise, dear sweet promise! How long we've waited to embrace our Cintia's dinners, breakfasts, suppers, and in-between-times meals! And to devour with passion her leeks, her vegetables, her tender meats, her white wines and her red wines, her stews, her pastries and her dear sweet love!

He turns to the audience and points to where he was.

Everybody, look! Look at poor Arlecchino! Drawn, wasted, starved for food, starved for the love of the kitchen queen, starved, too, for a good joke on somebody. He hasn't tricked anyone for weeks. His mind is wasting. He's thought of nothing but a few little pranks—making the old doctor pull out all his fingernails to save himself forever from the plague, making the old merchant eat a bowl of mud from the bottom of the river to get back his youthful appetites—little things, hardly worth mentioning. Arlecchino will surely die of waste, wasting away for the want of a meal, wasting away for the want of a prank, wasting away for the want of that foul, beautiful, exquisite, dirty, queenly, wretched, tender, powerful, tasteful, tasty, toothsome, loathsome, lovesome, likesome, wantsome, needsome Cintia! Everybody, weep!

A great voice from CINTIA'S *door shouts, "Out, out!" and a pot is flung through the door as* COVIELLO *is hurtled onto the stage floor.*

SCENE 2

COVIELLO. Oh, you there—man! Help me. You are a friend?
ARLECCHINO. I am, I am that if nothing else.

COVIELLO. You are a fellow man?

ARLECCHINO. A fellow man.

COVIELLO. Fellow man, do you know what I am?

ARLECCHINO. You are a bird.

COVIELLO. I am a husband! Coviello, the husband!

ARLECCHINO. Friend, tell me—what sort of a bird is a husband?

COVIELLO. What indeed? What is he but the chattel of a wife, who is given beatings for his charity and mercy——

ARLECCHINO. And maggoty meat for his dinner.

COVIELLO. Whose love and faithfulness is rewarded with slander, suspicion, lying and being found out——

ARLECCHINO. And who gets no dinner because of it.

COVIELLO. Who feels in one day all the tortures of all the martyrs in the Pope's book——

ARLECCHINO. And who gets nothing to eat at the end of it.

COVIELLO. Whose body is full of bruises, his head full of shouts and commands, his heart full of grief and despair——

ARLECCHINO. And only his belly is empty.

COVIELLO. Who is accused of living like a bishop, loving like an abbé, singing and laughing all day like a monk, and does he? No——

ARLECCHINO. No! He fasts and starves like an anchorite!

COVIELLO. Then will you, my friend, help me in my vow of abstinence? Witness that, from this time forth, Coviello will abstain from wives, from all wives—all but one.

ARLECCHINO. Ah, of course—Cintia.

COVIELLO. Flaminia!

ARLECCHINO. Who?

COVIELLO. Flaminia, of course, Flaminia!

ARLECCHINO. But—but you have abstained from all wives.

COVIELLO. All wives, all! All but one—Pantalone's. Ah, Pantalone's wife is not a wife.

ARLECCHINO. Not your wife.

COVIELLO. She is not a wife, she is an elegant repast, a savor of fine living, a dinner cooked for the celebration of the archduke's only daughter's betrothal to the cardinal's favorite mistress's son. Flaminia is the vapor of the white wine, the aroma of the salads, the sauce of the meats, the nectar of the fruits—no, they are all too gross for Flaminia! She is the distillation of the vapor, the swoon of the aroma, the sauciness of the sauce, the aphrodisiac of the nectar!

ARLECCHINO. Come—I will help you eat her.

COVIELLO. Not so fast, my friend. First we must dispose of the old goat Pantalone.

ARLECCHINO. Ah, leave the disposal of the husbands to me.

COVIELLO. Oh, that is my friend! If you do that for me, I make you a great promise.

COVIELLO *becomes solemn.*

If we get Flaminia alone with me, we will share in my harvest.

ARLECCHINO, *incredulous.* Share?

COVIELLO. Yes, dearest friend. Pantalone is a rich man, a very rich man. And Flaminia keeps his keys. I promise you that once I have spent the night with Flaminia, you, my dear friend, will be rewarded well with anything that Pantalone owns.

ARLECCHINO. Anything?

COVIELLO. From the bottom of my heart.

ARLECCHINO. A promise!

COVIELLO. A promise!

COVIELLO *knocks at* FLAMINIA'S *door.*

ARLECCHINO. There goes the old goat Coviello doing in the old goat Pantalone. Oh these old bearded geldings with all their manhood dangling from their spittle and their chins!

COVIELLO. Holla! Flaminia!

ARLECCHINO. Holla! Flaminia! His voice cracking like a boy's of thirteen, hawking wares he hasn't got, crying promises he can't pay.

COVIELLO. Holla, Flaminia!

ARLECCHINO. Holla, Flaminia! He'll spend the night! Up until midnight. And then he wraps the winding sheet on again and goes back to Hell. Eh, Coviello! Ghost! Gelding!

COVIELLO. She doesn't answer, comrade!

ACT I, SCENE 2

ARLECCHINO. Knock again, love!

Continuing to himself.

Knock, and when we get Flaminia alone with you, we get Cintia alone with me, eh, palsy? I swear if I didn't love your kitchen slop so that I have no mind for any woman but her, I could love Pantalone's banquet just to spite you, you lame unicorn, twice in a single night.

Suddenly ARLECCHINO *jumps to one side of himself, and begins to sneer at the figure he cuts.*

Look at you, Arlecchino, bragging of loving two in a single night! Which of them would have you? Would any? You lying, stinking, starving, cheating, whining, shrinking little exclamation point! I saw you at the fair, remember, when you made love to the farmer's wife, and the old sow she was selling fell on her back in her litter and laughed herself to death.

Proudly, concealing his chagrin, he answers himself.

I? I? You mistake me, whoever you are, for some lovesick Arlecchino. Look again, sir, look, and may you die of awe and wonder, may you be racked in Hell with the special torments they have there for the jealousy of Arlecchino, look at me once, strike yourself dumb and blind, stumble into the nearest ditch, die and join the damned writhing with the jealousy of me. And remember Arlecchino, the lover of a thousand conquests, for all his fat belly.

He whips around and, squinting, looks hard for the man he described.

Where? Where? I make out only a thin wavy line. What is it? A wisp of smoke? A visible breath of foul air? Or the dangling string of a hurried sneeze?

He rises to his full towering self and directs the seeker.

Shut your eyes, shut your eyes and turn around this way. And when you open them, may you be struck dumb at once by the radiance of my visible passion, my easily read ardor, and my audibly heroic manly mold!

He shuts his eyes, gropes his way until he faces about, braces himself, and looks. He controls himself for a moment, then pointing at the figure he cuts, he looses a hideous yawp of a laugh, and cries:

That!

Wheeling about, he slaps himself hard in the face and says, deeply wounded:

Beast!

COVIELLO. Come, come quickly. She is opening the door.

FLAMINIA *appears from her house.* ARLECCHINO, *overcome by her beauty, gasps and drops into* COVIELLO's *arms.*

SCENE 3

FLAMINIA. Ardent, ardent Coviello!

COVIELLO, *with* ARLECCHINO *resting in his arms.* Angel Flaminia!

FLAMINIA. Ah! What is that frightful bundle you are holding? Ah-h! Is it a dead beast?

COVIELLO. No, no, my angel, don't be frightened. You see, it is only a man. It is my friend, who has come from heaven to help us, angel. He did not mean to frighten you. Did you mean to frighten my angel, my friend?

ARLECCHINO, *still dangling.* I did not mean to frighten his angel, my angel. Did I mean to frighten my angel, his friend? No, no, his friend did not mean to frighten his angel, his angel.

FLAMINIA. Is he out of his mind, Coviello?

COVIELLO. No, my dear, he is here to help us. Will you forgive him?

FLAMINIA. Anything, anything but another night with Pantalone. As my sweet Coviello knows, I abide by custom, decorum, and so on, but always—Flaminia confesses her fault—she has been a slave to fashion. As the world knows, the fashion has not yet been born that has escaped me, none has left me more than two days behind, or just time enough to get at my husband's chest when he was asleep and into the shops when he was away. I confess it, yes, it was my sin. Now, now it has become my penance. In what mad turn of fashion did it become fashionable for young girls to marry old men? And why had the fashion come to me just when I turned the fashionable age to marry? It has undone me, twice over it has undone me. For now that the fashion for two whole weeks has dictated that wives be virtuous, I have made a solemn vow to break with it. Coviello, help me be brave and true to my oath.

COVIELLO. Oh, my frail innocence, trust in me. I will help you be true to your vow. And here is the ideal friend who has promised to help me help you keep your vow to break your vow.

FLAMINIA. And I can trust him?

COVIELLO. My honesty, as you can trust in me.

FLAMINIA. Walk off a moment, dear Coviello, let me speak to him.

COVIELLO *walks off.* FLAMINIA *beckons to* ARLECCHINO.

Dear friend. Come close to me.

ARLECCHINO *approaches her shufflingly, stands before her, hangdog with embarrassment.*

What is your name?

ARLECCHINO. Arlecchino.

FLAMINIA. Dear Arlecchino, would you—could you—help me?

ARLECCHINO *falls to his knees with a moan and almost grabs the hem of her gown to kiss it.*

FLAMINIA, *in the tone of a woman who has mastered the art of saying, "Don't!"* Ardent, ardent Arlecchino!

ARLECCHINO. Gracious banquet, ask anything, anything of me.

FLAMINIA. Then you will help me undo my husband?

ARLECCHINO. Fair aroma, he and any other.

FLAMINIA. And you will get Coviello into my house tonight?

ARLECCHINO. This night or any other, tender meat, this or any other.

FLAMINIA, *more surprised than outraged.* Tender meat!

ARLECCHINO. Forgive me, I was dreaming of a feast.

FLAMINIA. So!

ARLECCHINO. But I can content myself with its fragrance. If I am promised that, I will help another man to dine his fill.

FLAMINIA. Ah, you dear, clever tradesman! If you can but think of a way to get Coviello into the house, you shall have meat of me as well as fragrance.

ARLECCHINO. Meat of you!

FLAMINIA. A banquet, everything that lies in my power to spread before you.

ARLECCHINO. Then I will help the young pheasant to an old onion, and win for myself, if I understand aright, at least a bit of the dessert?

FLAMINIA, *graciously extending her hand.* A promise.

ARLECCHINO, *gallantly taking it.* A promise! Coviello, here is our plan!

COVIELLO, *joyfully.* Everything is arranged?

ARLECCHINO. Everything is arranged.

COVIELLO. Loyal friend!

ARLECCHINO. Both of you are to pretend that Arlecchino is mute, and that he is a country cousin of Coviello's. When we meet Pantalone, be aghast at the foul odor of his breath and urge him to see a dentist.

COVIELLO. But how am I to get into Pantalone's house tonight?

ARLECCHINO. Ah, an old man is a natural fool. Nothing is easier. For instance, let Flàminia make it known to him that his son and heir is on the way.

FLAMINIA. What? Then the old fool will never leave my side, dote on me night and day, give me things to suck, pillows to lie on, and wait on me with the devotion of a profligate son standing with pen and parchment over his father's deathbed.

ARLECCHINO. That I should live to teach a woman womanly wisdom! Little pheasant, until the heir is apparent—which, Heaven bless old Pantalone however it will, can never be for him—the cold stone of an ancient husband is as a pebble in the hands of a young wife. Want this and that. Need things here and there. Command night and morning. Bring him near, send him far. He comes into the presence, dismiss him. Dismissed, recall him. His friends, the merchants, are at your door? You need solitude. Your friends, the comedians, are in the square? You need bustle, excitement, noise, distraction. From morning to night you cry after him: Pantalone, for my salvation and your own delight, lie with me tonight. From night to morning, you whisper hoarsely as though the convulsion is overtaking you: Pantalone, Pantalone, if you love your wife and your own posterity, sleep on the carpet in the other room. Begin with lemons.

FLAMINIA. Lemons?

ARLECCHINO. You need lemons, you dote on them. You have the taste for lemons, and would he be so niggardly a father that he would deny you harmless little lemons? Father, says Pantalone, FATHER! Honest Flaminia, can you find it in your virtue to fool the old fool from there?

FLAMINIA. Honest Arlecchino, you are a masterpiece!

COVIELLO. My friend, my friend!

The morning coughing and wheezing of old PANTALONE *is heard within.* ARLECCHINO *jumps from the house in surprise.*

ARLECCHINO. Do you keep horses in the very house of so wealthy a merchant as Pantalone?

FLAMINIA. Horses? What horses?

The wheezing is heard again.

ARLECCHINO. Ah no. It is the cook tossing the swill into the canal from the other side of the house.

FLAMINIA. It is swill, and it is going into the canal, but it is not the cook who is tossing it in.

ARLECCHINO. Who, then?

FLAMINIA, *at the door, with tragic dignity.* My husband, when he rises in the morning, goes to the window overlooking the canal—

She shudders.

to clear his throat.

She goes into the house.

SCENE 4

COVIELLO, *almost in tears.* Save her, my friend, save her from that old man.

ARLECCHINO. You remember your promise?

COVIELLO. Yes, yes, what shall I do now?

ARLECCHINO. Stand away from the door, and as Pantalone comes out, I will meet him.

COVIELLO. But he does not know you.

ARLECCHINO, *laughing.* He will know me soon enough.

SCENE 5

The door opens and PANTALONE *comes out.* ARLECCHINO *has assumed the attitude of a beggar standing at his door for alms. He says nothing, pretending to be mute, but approaches* PANTALONE *and signifies his dire poverty and the old merchant's opportunity to store up good deeds for salvation.*

PANTALONE, *glowers at him and barks into his face.* What are you doing here? Is this a house of God that you should beg before my door?

ARLECCHINO, *getting a whiff of* PANTALONE's *breath in this outburst, sails back across the stage, and falls into* COVIELLO's *arms like an asphyxiated bird.*

Coviello, what is the matter with the beggar?

COVIELLO. Beggar! My good friend Pantalone, this is my good friend Arlecchino, my country cousin who has come to visit.

PANTALONE. Have I offended him then?

COVIELLO. Arlecchino! Arlecchino! Stand up and greet our good friend Pantalone.

ARLECCHINO *points to* PANTALONE *and pretends to cry.*

Pantalone wants to know if he has offended you.

ARLECCHINO *moans.*

Stop bawling, Arlecchino, and you will have his apology from his own mouth.

ARLECCHINO *moans even louder and tries to run away.*

With his own breath——

ARLECCHINO *breaks loose and runs behind* COVIELLO *to hide.*

Forgive him, Pantalone. Cousin Arlecchino is beloved by his country neighbors, he has a good heart, and he's the merriest of the village idiots.

ARLECCHINO *takes a moment to digest this injury.*

PANTALONE. Merriest? Ah, a little joke. Ha, ha! You see, Pantalone can laugh at an idiot as well as any man. Ha, ha, ha!

And he laughs directly into COVIELLO's *face. Stiff as a board,* COVIELLO *falls face forward against* PANTALONE's *chest.*

What is the matter with you? Coviello, were you merry in the village too?

COVIELLO. That breath—— Oh, that breath——

ARLECCHINO *runs up to him and pulls his sleeve. He motions vigorously toward his own mouth and shakes his head wildly.*

Cousin Arlecchino says that is not breath!

ARLECCHINO *mimes swallowing a savory morsel, falls dead, sits up, studies* PANTALONE, *and then as though coming to a decision, shakes his head slowly.* PANTALONE *looks to* COVIELLO *for translation of this.*

Cousin Arlecchino says that dead men stuffed with garlic wouldn't smell like that.

PANTALONE, *lurches toward them, outraged.* Stuffed with garlic!

ARLECCHINO *motions toward them to attend his next charade, extends a hand toward* PANTALONE, *as if to say, "Tell me, Pantalone," jumps into a handspring, and eases himself down on his head.*

COVIELLO, *shouting to* PANTALONE *and getting ready for flight with* ARLECCHINO. Cousin Arlecchino wants to know, when you were talking to him were you standing on your head?

ARLECCHINO, *reinforcing* COVIELLO's *translation with attentive nods, is patting his backside.*

Because Cousin Arlecchino thinks——

PANTALONE, *starting after them, raging.* Idiots! What does the idiot cousin think?

COVIELLO, *while he and* ARLECCHINO *are running.* Cousin Arlecchino thinks——

FLAMINIA *appears at the door.*

SCENE 6

FLAMINIA, *with mock horror, since her husband has stopped dead two inches from her.* Ardent, ardent Pantalone!

PANTALONE, *turning aside, to himself.* Oh, my plague!

FLAMINIA, *indignantly, to* PANTALONE. Have you taken to beating your friends in the streets? Why? Have they offended you?

Then, indignantly to the other two.

Have you offended my dear husband Pantalone?

PANTALONE. Yes, yes, they have abused the dignity of my middle age!

FLAMINIA. How? In what way? Tell me, and we will make a public scandal of them.

PANTALONE. No, no, it is a private matter. Hardly anything——
Aside.

Public scandal indeed! One in our household is enough!
To FLAMINIA.

It was nothing, nothing at all——

FLAMINIA, *fanning herself.* I am faint—— Ugh—— Help me, I am falling.

PANTALONE, *runs to her, and* FLAMINIA *screams and retreats from him. Furious, he blurts out*: What is the matter with

ACT I, SCENE 6

me? Tell me, Flaminia, before I walk through the streets this morning.

FLAMINIA. No, no, it is nothing, nothing at all.

PANTALONE. Nothing at all! I have cut down three people in three minutes just by opening my mouth and you say it is nothing at all. What is the matter with me? Am I the plague? Am I the Last Messenger?

FLAMINIA. Stand away, Pantalone—over there. Open your mouth—— Wide—wider——

The three of them rise on their toes and peer into PANTALONE'S *mouth from across the stage. They groan and shake their heads.* FLAMINIA *begins to weep as though widowed.*

PANTALONE, *anxiously.* What is it?

To ARLECCHINO.

What do you see?

ARLECCHINO *points to his mouth.*

COVIELLO. Cousin Arlecchino says: teeth!

PANTALONE. Teeth! Teeth! Of course he saw teeth! Did he expect to see scythes and hourglasses?

ARLECCHINO *mimes taking out his teeth one by one.*

COVIELLO. Cousin Arlecchino says when your teeth come out, then the smell will go too.

PANTALONE. Must they come out?

ARLECCHINO, *arms crossed, stamps his foot.*

COVIELLO. They must.

PANTALONE. How many must I lose?

ARLECCHINO *mimes grasping all his teeth in his fist and pitching them on the floor.*

COVIELLO. All.

PANTALONE, *elaborately tragic.* Suddenly I have become old.
The other three register surprise at this intelligence.

FLAMINIA, *running to him.* Ah, my Paolo, my Hercules, my Pan—old? Hercules old? A bacchant old? No, no, no, no, no!
Waggling one finger under PANTALONE'S *nose, with her other hand she is motioning* COVIELLO *into the house.*
ARLECCHINO, *who has caught the signal, is prodding*

COVIELLO *on. When they get to the door,* ARLECCHINO *opens it with the unhurried aplomb of a rich man's porter and bows* COVIELLO *in.*

Can a few teeth change a man's passion? Can a husband's virtues be undone in the mouth? Pantalone, Pantalone, what curious discerning woman was ever put off by a mumble? For me my Apollo will shine with or without his teeth. I will find a dentist for you, Achilles!

PANTALONE. How can I thank you enough, my Iphigenia?

ARLECCHINO, *aside to* FLAMINIA. Get to the lemons, Clytemnestra.

FLAMINIA, *as* PANTALONE *has begun to walk off.* Pantalone! Come here to me!

PANTALONE. A command! Are you commanding me, Helen?

FLAMINIA. When you return today, you will bring me some lemons.

PANTALONE. I? I will bring you lemons? I, Agamemnon? I, Achilles?

FLAMINIA, *imperiously.* I, Diana, will have lemons! I have a craving for them, I dote on them, I NEED lemons, and will you be so niggardly a father that you will deny me harmless little lemons?

PANTALONE. Anchises bearing lemons home from battle! A father bringing the gift of lemons—FATHER!

He gapes at FLAMINIA *for a moment, then throws out his arms to her.*

HECUBA!

FLAMINIA. My dear——

PANTALONE, *beside himself.* You shall have lemons! An armful of lemons, a bushel! No, a chest, a chest! All the lemons in the stalls will be yours. Pantalone—father Pantalone—will drag the chest through the streets himself! Tonight, Flaminia, lemons will be at your feet!

FLAMINIA. And they will be ripe, Pantalone?

PANTALONE. Ripe! Ripe! A father will bring ripe lemons!

FLAMINIA. And in a chest? A large chest?

PANTALONE. In a chest! Ripe! Ripe! A father!

ACT I, SCENE 7

FLAMINIA. And you will lock the lemons in a chest?
PANTALONE. A father will lock them in a chest!—Ripe! Ripe!
—Tonight—lemons—a ripe father—locked in a chest!
He runs out.

SCENE 7

ARLECCHINO. You have your lemons tonight, Flaminia?
FLAMINIA. Dear Arlecchino!
ARLECCHINO. And I my meat?
FLAMINIA. A promise!
ARLECCHINO. A promise!
She extends her hand to him regally, he takes it royally, and they go in.

SCENE 8

PANTALONE, *returning in haste.*

Flaminia, there is something I have forgotten to tell you! Where are you?—Oh, what news, what news to celebrate! —Ah, she is gone! Flaminia, dearest mother! Dearest, dearest Flami— Plague on her, let her go! Her news put me off entirely. And I had meant to tell her before I left that I would not be home at all tonight, for my business is calling me elsewhere. Well, she will have her lemons, I'll bring the chest. And then, to business! Oh, that business is a comfort to a man's heart when he is plagued with the coquetry of a young wife who has eyes for everyone but her husband. An honest wife is what a fair husband needs. And Pantalone, you have found her!—if that plague my coquette whom I took for a wife doesn't find me out. I'll call her, my Franceschina, that good woman with the honest tongue, and if she can get rid of her husband tonight, Pantalone will celebrate his new fatherhood with an enviable try for another son. Ah, Zanni, what a lucky man you are to have such a woman as Franceschina to bear you sons, and such a man as Pantalone to provide them for you.

He goes to FRANCESCHINA'S *house.*

Franceschina, Franceschina, your fond merchant Pantalone is here with his wares. Franceschina, come out and have a look at your purchase. Come out, good Franceschina, and together we will drive a hard bargain.

SCENE 9

FRANCESCHINA *comes out of her house. She bawls at the top of her voice with great joy at seeing him.*

FRANCESCHINA. Pantalone, my sweet lover and my impotent husband's cuckolder, how are you?

PANTALONE. Not so loud, good Franceschina——

FRANCESCHINA, *still shouting.* When can we be in bed again together? Can you be rid of your harlot wife tonight and taste the joys of an honest woman's love, or is your painted slut so malicious that she will tie you like a dog to the foot of her bed to keep you virtuous and in sight while she romps all night with lewd actors and mountebanks before your very eyes?

PANTALONE. Good Franceschina, I know how evil evil appears in your eyes.

FRANCESCHINA. Bawdry is my abomination.

PANTALONE. But a little deceit now and then is the salt of love.

FRANCESCHINA. Deceit! Let a deceiver near me and I will crush his bones. Ah, my protector Pantalone, never speak to me of deceivers!

PANTALONE. Sh! Franceschina, we had better whisper than shout, eh! Zanni may hear us.

FRANCESCHINA. Don't trouble about Zanni! Zanni is too deaf to hear even his wife, too blind to see even a lover, and too old to be even a husband. I am proud I need conceal nothing from him.

PANTALONE. Then tonight I will be with you, good woman, and there will be nothing to hinder us. Before I come, we will send a sign, a message that we are free.

FRANCESCHINA. Make it plain and honest, Pantalone. No deceitful lover's notes. I hate a deceitful message.

PANTALONE. Till tonight, virtue!

FRANCESCHINA. Till tonight, centaur!

PANTALONE *goes out, and* FRANCESCHINA *goes into her house.*

SCENE 10

ARLECCHINO *comes out of* FLAMINIA'S *house in a fury.*

ARLECCHINO. Curse her innocence! Curse her virtuous beauty! And curse that decaying lecher Coviello! She gave me meat! Meat! Am I starving or am I a starving man? Ah, your promise, says Coviello. First your promise to our good friend Arlecchino. No, no, says Arlecchino, let that go now for a while. Arlecchino can wait. Wait, says Coviello, my friend wait? My own Flaminia, have you Pantalone's keys? I have. Can you get at his stores at once? I can. Have you dined, Flaminia, my purity? I have. Has the household dined? The household, says Arlecchino, have we made promises to the household? The cook, says Coviello, the footmen, the servants, the seamstress, the gardener, the porter, the messenger, the coachman, the scullery maids, the kitchen boys and the stableboys? They have, says Flaminia, dined their fill. And the monkey, says Coviello, the monkey in your blessed boudoir. Has he been nourished? Is he content? He is, says Flaminia. Content, full, yawning, and ready to sleep. Then bring a platter, says Coviello, bring a platter for our devoted friend. All, all the rest, says he, is yours. Take, partake, eat, sup, repast.

ARLECCHINO *mimes the great platter being brought before*

him by FLAMINIA. *He mimes searching the great surface of the platter, setting it on the ground, putting his nose closer and closer to its immaculate surface, and at last finding a minute particle on it which might be edible. He lifts it in his hands with great care lest it drop and disappear, and says to them, as though overwhelmed by their bounty:*

For me? A promise, says Flaminia. Good-by, says Coviello,

And ARLECCHINO *imitates his weeping.*

never shall we forget. Never, never. Good-by, dear friend. Good-by.

And he mimes COVIELLO's *shutting the door firmly on the last good-by.*

Arlecchino, you clever, clever, clever lover! Arlecchino the rogue! Arlecchino the trickster! Everybody, look! Look at Arlecchino! Only Arlecchino is clever enough to be cuckolded without even having a wife!

Suddenly he turns on himself and begins to address himself again.

Come, Arlecchino, can you sing with the lovers? No! Then growl with the husbands. Join with the cuckolds and you will have your revenge.

Shouting at the top of his voice.

Pantalone! Thieves are in your house! Come. Come quickly! Pantalone, Pantalone, they are stealing your treasures. Come, Pantalone, save your meat! If you don't hurry, we'll be calling you by other names! Do you want other names? Other names, Pantalone!

SCENE 11

ZANNI *comes out of his house. In a small plaintive voice, he asks with innocent curiosity.*

ZANNI. Are you calling my neighbor Pantalone?

ARLECCHINO. Hello! Who is this bag of wrinkles?

To ZANNI.

Venerable old gentleman, do you know where I can find Pantalone?

ZANNI. Venerable? Do you call me venerable? A man with his blood raging for his posterity? Pantalone is venerable, call him an old gentleman, not a man with a quick step and a clear eye!

ARLECCHINO, *aside.* Oho! A sprightly cadaver! What does this rosy babe want with his posterity? Oh, Arlecchino, a perfect customer! To business!

To ZANNI.

Young man, look at me. Do you see me?

ZANNI, *who is facing the other way.* Why should I not? Of course I see you! Ask Pantalone the mole if he is blind, not Zanni the eagle!

ARLECCHINO. But what do you see? Only Arlecchino! My child, under Arlecchino's vanities and frills

In a whisper to ZANNI.

there lies concealed a practitioner!

ZANNI. A man of the science?

ARLECCHINO. Of *the* science, friend, *the* science. Only now I was calling Pantalone on a medical matter.

ZANNI. Poor man, he is dropping into the grave, I know.

With commiseration.

Is he dying?

ARLECCHINO. No, no, it was not his death but his birth I was to tell him about. Pantalone has just been delivered of a son.

ZANNI. He-he! That ancient monument? Impossible!

ARLECCHINO. I have delivered a son to Pantalone that is a solemn tribute to the father!

ZANNI. That fallow unicorn? That worn-through shoe? How could it be?

ARLECCHINO. A son that will be his heir, his posterity, his future!

ZANNI. Oh, that discarded calendar, that yesterday's gossip, that dry dug! How could he beget a child?

ARLECCHINO. Through the magic of Dr. Arlecchino's science!

ZANNI. That alone?

ARLECCHINO. And the help of Pantalone's wife, of course. As a medical confidence, young man, let me tell you that Flaminia is a great aid in begetting a son.

ZANNI. That is all very well for Flaminia, but my wife is too lazy to do anything, and in fact—in strictest confidence of course to the esteemed doctor—it is not my fault at all that we have no child, but Franceschina's.

ARLECCHINO. Well, well, perhaps, but the malady senectatis has been known since Galen's time to be the worst betrayer of a man's productivity.

ZANNI. Yes, you would think so, and never would I contradict the learned doctor—and all appearances would point to it too: I, wise, matured, and—let me admit it quite frankly—a little past the first bloom—and Franceschina, young, lusty, the darling of the world, a sweet pouting apple if ever one lived. But it is she, she, not Zanni, the most willing and able of husbands, who keeps children from us. Never was there so lazy a creature as Franceschina. Would you believe it, good doctor—a confidence, you understand, since no one lives who suspects—sometimes you would think she had reason not to lust for my manhood.

ARLECCHINO, *astonished*. For *your* manhood? She does not lust for you? What reason, Zanni?

ZANNI, *shaking his head with the old perplexity*. Who can say what is in a woman's mind?

ARLECCHINO. Zanni, I have the cure! Pantalone's cure! Dr. Arlecchino will dig a son out of the very earth! Is it agreed that I can use your wife?

ZANNI, *joyfully*. Use her, use her, good doctor!

ARLECCHINO. Perfect husband! Then quickly, Zanni, bring a spade——

ZANNI. A spade——

ARLECCHINO. A rope——

ZANNI. A rope——

ARLECCHINO. And a great basket to carry the child into the house.

ZANNI, *amazed*. Will she beget it here?

ARLECCHINO. Here and nowhere else.

ZANNI, *rejoicing.* Today I will be a father too!

ARLECCHINO. Call your wife, bring the basket, and we will begin.

ZANNI, *running to his door.* Franceschina! Franceschina! Come out! This good doctor is going to give you a child!

SCENE 12

FRANCESCHINA *comes out bellowing.*

FRANCESCHINA. Why are you calling me, you decayed cheese, you sunken vessel? What stupidity is exciting you now?

ZANNI. Worthless! Worthless lazy plum of a young, tantalizing, unrewarding female! You will thank your husband yet, who is good enough to bless you with a child with the help of this good doctor who is standing before you now.

FRANCESCHINA. That!

She starts to leave.

ZANNI. Come back! Come back, unnatural woman, and listen to the doctor, do you hear!

ARLECCHINO. Listen to the doctor, good Franceschina, after your husband has gone for the basket.

FRANCESCHINA, *catching the note in his voice, stands and looks at him fixedly.*

Dr. Arlecchino, good wife, humble practitioner and master minister to a woman's needs, will explain to you what a blessing in disguise has come to you this day.

ZANNI. Listen to the doctor, follow his instructions to the letter, and though you do not deserve it, he will get you a child.

ZANNI *goes into the house for the basket.*

SCENE 13

FRANCESCHINA, *bawls out directly to* ARLECCHINO *without a moment's hesitation.* A blessing in disguise is a lover. There is no other for a woman, and if you—who are no more a doctor than my husband—are an honest lover who is lying his way into my house, say so at once, take off your disguise, give me a chance to vouch for your blessing, and I will get you into my bed before my idiot husband is out of the house. If you are, then say the one word yes. If not, I will beat you down the street, have you hung for an impostor, a charlatan, an obscene betrayer of honest wives looking for plain lovers, and a cheater of woman's hopes. What is your answer?

ARLECCHINO, *overwhelmed.* Bountiful wife——

FRANCESCHINA, *ready to strike.* What is your answer?

ARLECCHINO, *quickly.* Yes, yes, yes!

FRANCESCHINA. Then hide in the basket that you tell the old fool will hold the child. He will carry it into the house, deposit it beside my bed, and after I have abused him for a clumsy idiot and locked him out, you will come out of the basket and give me your entire blessing. And remember, none of your tricks!

ARLECCHINO. A promise!

FRANCESCHINA. A promise!

SCENE 14

ZANNI *comes out of the house with the basket.*

ZANNI. Here is everything you called for, worthy doctor. Is there anything else I need to dig for the child?

ARLECCHINO. It is not you who digs, Zanni, but your wife.

ZANNI. And what should Zanni do while she digs?

ARLECCHINO. Spin.

ZANNI. A miracle! A miracle is coming to pass! That men should be taken out of earth, out of dust! Oh, the wonders of Medicine!

ARLECCHINO. And Latin too, Zanni, Medicine and Latin together. Do you have no faith in Latin?

ZANNI. Do you take me for Pantalone? Latin too, of course. Every wise man knows that, together, Latin and Medicine can make all things come to pass. Why, they have made men out of beasts——

ARLECCHINO. And beasts out of men——

ZANNI. Wise men out of fools——

ARLECCHINO. And fools out of wise men——

ZANNI. Truth out of error——

ARLECCHINO. And error out of truth——

ZANNI. Children out of dust——

ARLECCHINO. And dust out of children.

ZANNI. Dig, dig, Franceschina!

ARLECCHINO. And the Devil bless our enterprise!

FRANCESCHINA *begins to dig in the ground.*

Repeat after me, Franceschina: *Ignei, aerii, aquatani*——

FRANCESCHINA. *Ignari, alii, aquitinale*——

ZANNI. *Aquatani!*

FRANCESCHINA. *Aquitinale*——

ARLECCHINO. *Spiritus, salvete!*

FRANCESCHINA. *Spinatyphus, salvete!*

ARLECCHINO. *Spiritus, spiritus!* The Devil would blush at your Latin! *Spiritus,* Franceschina!

FRANCESCHINA, *thundering. Spinatyphus, salvete!*

ARLECCHINO. *Inferni ardentis monarcha*——

FRANCESCHINA. *Inferi adamas, monarcha*——

ZANNI. *Inferni ardentis!* Or your child will be stone! Say *inferni ardentis*, before the fires go out!

ARLECCHINO. *Propitiamus vos*——

FRANCESCHINA. *Propitiamus vos*——

ARLECCHINO. *Ut surgat Mephistophilis.*

FRANCESCHINA. *Ut surgat ma spinatyphus.*

From the hole that FRANCESCHINA *is digging, there is suddenly heard a cry of OUCH! after a particularly sharp lunge.*

ZANNI, *jumping to the hole and digging furiously.* We are blessed!

From the hole he has dug, some small stones come flying out onto the stage floor.

Look, look, Doctor. Franceschina, the little imp is playing already!

Shouting into the hole.

Wait, wait, my son, a few more blows and you're out!

He begins to dig like a madman. ARLECCHINO *grabs the rope from the basket and cries out to him.*

ARLECCHINO. The rope, the rope!

ZANNI *grabs the rope and shouts into the hole.*

ZANNI. Grab the rope, take hold of the rope, you little darling!

There is a growl from below like the roar of thunder.

Don't cry, little darling! Daddy is holding on!

Suddenly ZANNI *yells with fright and lunges into the hole head first, still hanging onto the rope.* FRANCESCHINA *and* ARLECCHINO *grab and pull,* ARLECCHINO *on* ZANNI'S *legs,* FRANCESCHINA *on* ARLECCHINO'S. *The tug of war goes back and forth, with* ZANNI *sometimes disappearing down to the ankles, sometimes emerging so that his face is visible for an instant before he goes down again. Finally, with a terrific yank on* FRANCESCHINA'S *part, they get* ZANNI *out of the hole, and the three of them lie sprawled on the stage floor. In the hole, his chin just clearing the ground, a blood-red* DEVIL *is looking out at them angrily. He folds his arms under his chin and rests them on the edge of the hole.*

DEVIL, *in a deep baritone.* Which of you had the strength to pull the Devil out of Hell?

ZANNI, *beside himself with joy, shouts.* A boy! It's a boy!

DEVIL. That old toad couldn't do it. And that wisp of straw

over there couldn't lift his eyes. Then it must have been the woman!

The DEVIL *gets very excited about this.*

What news this will be for Hell! What an event!

FRANCESCHINA. What news?

DEVIL. That a woman should stop the Devil in his work!

ZANNI. Child, give me your hand so that I can pull you out. Franceschina, bring the boy some swaddling clothes. Do you want him to freeze?

DEVIL. Pull me out? Come here and try, you old corpse.

ZANNI. What spirit! What a voice! Give me your hand, little angel!

ZANNI *grasps the* DEVIL'S *hand, and with his back to the hole, tugs it along the ground. The* DEVIL *remains calmly in the hole, watching as his hand detaches itself, and* ZANNI *puffs and pants with the weight of his burden. As he drags the arm.*

Oh, what a child! The little darling weighs more than his father! Are you all right, angel?

DEVIL. My toe is caught.

ZANNI. Don't worry, sweetheart. I'll have you out. Hang on!

The DEVIL *groans as though with the effort of being dragged.*

A little more, angel, just hold on a little longer.

DEVIL. There we are.

ZANNI. Ah, there we are. All out, sweetheart? All safe and sound?

He turns around, sees the detached arm in his grasp. With a shriek, he drops it.

Where's the rest of the child?

DEVIL. Here I am.

ZANNI. There you are, so you are. But I've pulled off his dear arm! How will he manage with one arm?

DEVIL. Oh, I'll manage.

ZANNI. My little angel has only one arm!

DEVIL, *bellowing.* I'll manage! Stop your wawling!

And he throws another arm at ZANNI *to make him stop.*

ZANNI, *almost knocked over by the arm, shrieks.* He's without arms! My angel has no arms!

DEVIL. Lots of arms, lots of arms—

And he throws arms out at ZANNI.

And legs, lots of legs—

And he throws three or four legs at ZANNI *for good measure.*

ZANNI, *at a loss as to how to manage this.* Franceschina, don't stand there gaping. Help me deliver our son before he throws away *all* his precious parts!

FRANCESCHINA. You're mad, you old fossil! Lunatic! Lunatic old Zanni!

ZANNI, *running to the* DEVIL, *grabs him about the head.* Monster mother! Look at your monster mother, darling, who won't even help your father bear his child! Both together now, darling! Heave ho!

DEVIL. Heave ho!

And the DEVIL'S *neck distends a couple of inches.*

ZANNI, *preparing for the second tug.* Heave ho!

DEVIL. Heave ho!

And the DEVIL'S *neck emerges a foot out of the hole.*

ZANNI. Once more and you're ours, child! Heave ho!

DEVIL. Heave ho!

And this time the DEVIL'S *head emerges five feet out of the hole and emits smoke through his mouth and ears.* ZANNI, *taking in the sight, faints dead away. The* DEVIL'S *head, in a flash, shoots down into the hole and disappears.*

FRANCESCHINA, *inspects* ZANNI, *and then, with a kick at his prostrate form.* Ach! Wake up the old fool and tell him the child is safe in the basket.

ARLECCHINO. And you remember your promise, madonna?

FRANCESCHINA. Agreed.

ARLECCHINO, *shaking* ZANNI *awake.* Zanni, Zanni, you can wake up now! The child has risen! Wake up, Zanni, wake up and sing the praises of the doctor!

ZANNI *wakes, crawls on all fours to the hole, and looks in.*

Quem quaeritis in caverno, O pater Zanni?
ZANNI. *Bambinum Franceschinum, O magicola.*
ARLECCHINO. *Non est hic; surrexit, sicut praedixero.*
ZANNI. Hallelujah! My child has risen!

He looks toward FRANCESCHINA *with gentle piety and asks*:
Franceschina, what is that sweet thing on thy knee?
FRANCESCHINA *makes ready to smite him, but* ARLECCHINO *interrupts.*

ARLECCHINO. Not there, Zanni! Our child is safe in the basket.
ZANNI. *Arlecchinum laudamus!* Let me see him! Let me see!
ARLECCHINO. No, no, the little darling is fast asleep.
ZANNI. Tell me, Doctor——
ARLECCHINO. Does something trouble you, father?
ZANNI. Did he seem a bit red in the face?
ARLECCHINO. No, he had, I thought, a kind of pallor.
ZANNI. And tall? Advise me, Doctor, can a child be born taller than his father?
ARLECCHINO. Would you give birth to a snail? The child born to Pantalone was a head taller than the old man.
ZANNI. A head taller! Then my child is a mite—a sickly little flea—and Pantalone will always laugh at me!
ARLECCHINO. Take my word for it, consecrated father, your child, with the help of Lucifer, is bigger than Pantalone's.
ZANNI. Ah, so—bigger than Pantalone's—he-he-he!—Franceschina, you good-for-nothing wife, I bore a child bigger than Pantalone's.

And, he-heing to himself, bursting with vanity, he announces to the world as he goes into the house:
Bigger than Pantalone's!

SCENE 15

ARLECCHINO. Ha! My darling Franceschina, did I play the doctor well?

FRANCESCHINA. If you can stop your lies and deceits for a moment, climb into the basket and that dolt, that imbecile will carry you into the house if Franceschina has to break his back to do it.

ARLECCHINO, *getting into the basket, happily.* And the promise, gentle wife, the promise. You will give as you promised to your honest lover?

FRANCESCHINA. Villain! Thief! Player with words! Didn't Franceschina say once she had something for her honest lover? Is there anyone still living who doubts Franceschina's word?

ARLECCHINO. Madonna! Does Arlecchino have the valor to doubt?

ARLECCHINO *closes the lid over his head.* ZANNI *comes scampering out with bags of money and jewels in his arms.*

SCENE 16

ZANNI. Where is the blessed doctor? A boon, a boon for the good man! Where has he gone, Franceschina?

FRANCESCHINA. The doctor played his last joke on the fiend of hell in delivering your child. A great devil came by and stuffed him into a basket, and another devil was pressed into shouldering the burden and carrying him to his last torment.

ZANNI. The good doctor spirited away? Ah, but he will fool them. Take my word for it, good-for-nothing, that devil will be sorry he carried that basket an inch from where it rested.

He turns to the basket to lift it.

Come, my little curer of old age. Into the house with you. Franceschina, for your own good if not for mine, help me lift our blessed little intruder.

FRANCESCHINA. Be careful of your bones, dray horse, be careful you don't crumble into powder as you lift him, and make him bump his precious bottom.

ACT I, SCENE 17

ZANNI, *lifting the basket on his back and walking to the door of his house.* He-he-he! Old Zanni delivered him once; he can deliver him again. Heave ho!

ARLECCHINO, *inside the basket, imitating the* DEVIL. Heave ho!

ZANNI. He-he-he! Oh, the weight, the precious weight of him!

FRANCESCHINA *follows him and holds up the back of the basket.* ARLECCHINO *opens the lid, throws his arms wide, and embraces* FRANCESCHINA *with abandoned sweeps of his arms while the two are bearing him into the house.*

Feel the weight of him, Franceschina!

FRANCESCHINA. I will, you dolt, I will!

ZANNI. And, good-for-nothing, he wants a mother's love. Fondle him, Franceschina, promise you will fondle him.

FRANCESCHINA. Go on, you fool, I have promised.

ZANNI. And he'll want strength. Suckle him, suckle him tenderly, Franceschina.

FRANCESCHINA. Long and tenderly, old ruin, long and tenderly.

ZANNI. And that envious old merchant will never laugh at me again, do you hear. Oh no, my precious burden is bigger than Pantalone's.

ARLECCHINO, *making the sign of horns over him and speaking in the* DEVIL's *voice.* Much bigger, much bigger.

ZANNI. He-he-he! Oh, what spirit. What a child.

They go into ZANNI's *house.*

SCENE 17

COVIELLO *comes out of* FLAMINIA's *house.*

COVIELLO. Zanni carrying a heavy basket! Is it possible? Never did I think he could still lift a crutch! Ah, Coviello! Zanni will be your friend. Why should not Zanni carry the chest into Pantalone's house? Surely the old fool will want to help me make a fool of the old fool Pantalone.

SCENE 18

ZANNI *comes merrily out of his house.*

ZANNI. Coviello, I am a happy man!

COVIELLO. My good friend Zanni, what has come over you?

ZANNI. My wife has just driven me from the house, thrown a box, a mirror and a shoe at me, and forbid me ever to return to her sight until I have cast off forty of my years, and I am the happiest man in the world.

COVIELLO. What husband would not be happy, Zanni, with such a loving forbid. Ah, where is such another wife who forbids as Zanni's wife forbids? Lucky Zanni, my good friend. Oh, that I could share your good fortune. I weep for your joy, Zanni, joy to you and to all husbands.

ZANNI, *affected, begins to weep too.* Joy to us all, eh, Coviello, joy to all husbands!

Both weeping, they embrace and give comfort to each other.

COVIELLO. Joy to all husbands in single blessedness.

ZANNI, *detaching himself.* No, no, no. It's not that. There is a secret joy which I cannot tell. It is a secret from Pantalone.

COVIELLO. Zanni, we are friends indeed. I have a secret from Pantalone I am bursting to share with you.

ZANNI, *incredulous.* You have?

COVIELLO. Yes, and you must help me. You must carry a chest for me as I just saw you carry one into your own house.

ZANNI. Is there a chest to be carried into your house too? Has that accursed doctor spawned a whole generation of children from hell?

COVIELLO. No, no, Zanni, not my house. Into Pantalone's house.

ZANNI. Then Pantalone could not carry his own burden into his house? And my burden was bigger than Pantalone's! Tell me, Coviello, is it true that Pantalone could not lift his own child?

COVIELLO, *aside*. Curse him, he's gone mad!

To ZANNI.

No, no, Zanni, not a child, a chest of lemons, lemons! Listen, Zanni, tonight Pantalone will bring a chest of lemons to his door which his wife entreated of him.

ZANNI. A chest of lemons! What would his wife want with a chest of lemons?

COVIELLO. That's it, Zanni, that's it! Flaminia has led the old mange to believe that he is going to have a son. And Pantalone is mad to satisfy her every craving. Her first demand was for lemons, which Pantalone, to give her her full measure of delight, is sending in a chest.

ZANNI, *dully*. But what delight will there be for Flaminia in the lemons?

COVIELLO. No, no, you old—dear friend, there will be no lemons in the chest.

ZANNI. But you just said——

COVIELLO, *shouting at him in a frenzy of impatience*. Coviello, Coviello will be in the chest! It is I Pantalone will furnish for his wife's delight!

ZANNI, *as comprehension finally seizes him*. In a chest! He-he-he!

Pointing at COVIELLO *and shouting at him through his paroxysms of joy.*

Lemons!—Lemons!—Coviello in Pantalone's chest!—He-he-he!

COVIELLO. And I have come to ask you if you will carry the chest into Pantalone's house.

ZANNI. For his wife's delight! He-he! Yes, yes—Zanni will carry the chest.

COVIELLO. And it pleases you, Zanni? My good friend!

He is on the verge of tears again.

ZANNI. Zanni has carried a chest before. And he will carry it again. He-he-he! For his wife's delight!

They go off together.

SCENE 19

LEANDRO *comes in. He puts one hand to his mouth and calls in a low voice to* CINTIA's *door.*

LEANDRO. Coo-ee-ee! Coo-ee-ee! Cintia! It is Leandro! Surely she hasn't forgotten my love. I must remind her.

Again to CINTIA's *house.*

Cintia! It is Leandro of the meadow calling. Cintia! Leandro, behind the bridge, when the tide came in and woke us? Leandro, Cintia! Leandro who jumped from your window with nothing concealed but his modesty! Leandro, who offered you his heart—which you almost took from him with a kitchen knife! Leandro, Leandro, Venus and Mars, with whom and for how long will you be in there consoling yourself for my loss?

ARLECCHINO, *storming out of* FRANCESCHINA's *house.* Oh, what form of a pest is this? Wait until he's gone, Leandro!

SCENE 20

ARLECCHINO. Something for a lover! Yes, which lover? Mercury Arlecchino, the messenger, the lackey! Arlecchino the puppy who runs with billet-doux between his teeth from lover to lover. From lover to lover! Here, says she, is something for my lover. Out of the basket, you lying doctor, you fraud, out of the basket and run with this to Pantalone. Why are you standing in the basket? What are you waiting for? A-A-H-H, she screams, did you come to tamper with my virtue? Out, out, you cheat, you filthy, lewd, designing man! You charlatan, you fraudulent alchemist, you devil's mate! Sorcerer, cheater, lecher, liar, out of the house of an honest woman! Run with this note to Pantalone, and never

ACT I, SCENE 20

let me hear that you broke a promise again! Straight to Pantalone, do you hear, deliverer! Franceschina does not forget your promises!

Again he opens wide the imaginary pocket in his clothing.

Pocket, here! A letter for you!

Suddenly astonished by what he sees in the pocket.

Pocket, is there room? Look at you, stuffed, bulging with promises! Was there ever a man who carried such a bundle of promises!

Pretends to lift them out one at a time as he studies them.

Why, look at this dinner from Flaminia, days and days of dainties, all she has in her power to spread before me. Poor promise!

He puts it back tenderly and takes another.

And here is one for robes and furred gowns, pearls and lapis lazuli, all the wealth of the rich merchant Pantalone, signed my "dearest friend Coviello." Ah, here is a lusty, bawdy, plain-spoken promise, to be had just for jumping into a basket, paid on delivery!

Looks at the promise with impatience and pitches it back.

What a bruised little promise you are! What's this one at the bottom?

As he looks at it, he begins to jump and tremble with delight.

Oh, look at this sweet little promise!

Slapping his head.

Arlecchino, you simple seeker for salvation, here is a darling little whisper of a promise that says, "Come back and we'll be quits with the old fool for what he has made us bear." Cintia, queen of the kitchen! Arlecchino will be a respectable, well-fed lover of an old man's wife yet! Cintia will be my salvation!

He runs with anticipatory delight to CINTIA's *door, and knocks loudly on it.*

Oh, Cintia! Open the door for my salvation! Come out, Cintia, your little conspirator is here! Vengeance, Cintia, sweet vengeance is calling you! Come out, you great enchanter of the stomach! Arlecchino is here, sly Arlecchino, to help you be quits with that husband!

SCENE 21

CINTIA, *through the door, her voice brays at* ARLECCHINO. Who is bawling like a vulgar fishwife for Cintia? Doesn't he know that I must have silence in my kitchen?

ARLECCHINO. We are plighted to conspiracy, dearest mustard-seed. Come out and see who it is.

A pot flies across the stage, missing ARLECCHINO.

CINTIA. Silence!

ARLECCHINO. Vinegar has puckered her temper. Try again, Arlecchino.

He moves to one side of the door.

But we had better get out of harm's way. Remember, pod? "Come back and together we'll be quits with the old fool?" Put down your ladle and open the door.

CINTIA, *coming out and recognizing* ARLECCHINO. *With no great joy, she says*: Ah, it's you. You've come back.

ARLECCHINO. And that's all? No more?

CINTIA. Welcome.

ARLECCHINO. We have a great plot, Cintia. Do you remember our plot?

CINTIA, *as* LEANDRO *appears and throws her a kiss, she cries with ardor.* Ah, you've come back. Welcome, my heaven, my joy, a thousand welcomes!

LEANDRO, *behind* ARLECCHINO, *puts his fingers to his lips.*

ARLECCHINO. My ecstasy! Now you remember!

CINTIA, *as* ARLECCHINO *attempts to embrace her.* Don't touch me, poltroon!

ARLECCHINO. Now what in the Devil's name has gotten into this stockpot? Have you forgotten our plan? Have you forgotten what we have suffered together? Cintia, have you forgotten your promise?

LEANDRO, *in unison with* ARLECCHINO, *is urging all his words on* CINTIA *in silence*.

CINTIA, *responding to* LEANDRO. Never! How can you accuse me? Have I ever loved as I have loved you? Have I known such tenderness with my winter, my husband? What do I spice when I spice my mutton but the dear remembrance of your saucy advances? What do I wring when I strangle chickens but my husband's neck? The wine of your laughter, the milk of your ardor, the oil of your tongue, are mixed with my memories and stir my blood, and the reek, the stench, the filth of my husband's glance, his word, his motion, his—ugh—I throw every day into the canal. Everything I beat, scatter, mash, poison and throw away is my husband's; and everything I store, treasure, fondle and keep in my heart is——

ARLECCHINO. Arlecchino! Blessed and happy man! You are beatified, sanctified, transmuted! No more tears, my poor Cintia, you have persuaded me! No more entreaty, I am won!

CINTIA. Are you in truth? Can I trust my heart?

ARLECCHINO. Forever and ever, my love!

CINTIA. And if I wait, if I tell you now when to come to me, you will come?

ARLECCHINO. Though twenty men were at your door when I came, my faithful Cintia, I and I alone will be at your side.

CINTIA. And if some stupid clown of a pretending lover bars your way, you will not be put off, you will not let him deceive you, my own?

ARLECCHINO. No stupid clown will bar love's way, my true and loving Cintia! Love, not clowning, passion, not tricks, will win you.

CINTIA. And if I ask some small, some little indignity of you that you may come and go as you please, so that we will not be detected or interrupted, so that you may come to my door at any time and even be admitted by my husband, so that never again need you ask assurance or wonder how to gain admittance, so that never again need a stupid conspiracy stand between us and the ecstasy of our pleasure, will you suffer this tiny indignity for our love?

ARLECCHINO. My heart is too full, dear Cintia, to mouth more promises. All, all, I promise to give to you eternally. What indignity would I not suffer for you now? You have given me the gift of perfect love.

CINTIA. Then tonight and forever after, as you please and without let or hindrance, disguise yourself as a dull clod of a girl and come to visit me with some little parcel, some small gift, and even my husband will know you well and trust you as my sweet, beguiling country cousin!

ARLECCHINO. Ah, love, not even Arlecchino could dream up a ruse at once so simple, so sure, and so eternally rewarding.

CINTIA. Then go now, my promised lover! No kiss, no touch, no word between us—until tonight!

LEANDRO *throws a kiss to her, he departs and* CINTIA *goes into her house.*

SCENE 22

ARLECCHINO. It was a dream, and never will I believe that such words were spoken to ragamuffin Arlecchino. But what a dream! After tonight, my heart, my soul, my stomach, and my pride will all be filled. Pocket, here! Take this tenderly. Hug Cintia's promise close to your sides. Don't tear, pocket. It's a very great and heavy promise, but hold it just until tonight. Because after tonight, pocket, after tonight— our cup runneth over!

He runs out with a bound.

ACT II

SCENE 1

ARLECCHINO *enters dressed as a woman.*

ARLECCHINO, *very feminine.* Oh, la, what a dish! Arlecchino, you're just a darling irresistible! And if you aren't the country cousin to end all country cousins.

He hoists his bodice so that he protrudes indecently and walks liquidly about the stage.

Kind gentleman, a kind word for a kind lady? La, la, la, that's a harsh word. You'd better just give me a kind look. Oh, la, that's a scowl. Settle a smile on your face, dear man, and give me a taste of a little kiss?

ARLECCHINO *puckers his mouth and closes his eyes in anticipation, then lurches back with a wee cry.*

Oh! A man can be such a beast! Now you see, Arlecchino, the secret of woman's virtue. Give her scorn for her love, and she is outraged to the point of virtue. Walk the paths of a furious virtue, Signora Arlecchino.

ARLECCHINO *yanks the bodice flat, and takes on the look of a too-old duenna.*

Don't touch me, you deliciously indecent man. If you come near me, you devilish temptation, you tasty morsel of sin, I'll scream, you impetuous fool, you non-stop daredevil, I'll call my lame husband, you hotheaded libertine, and he'll tell you to go away. Don't turn your back when I talk to you, don't run off when I'm repulsing you, you outrageous potency, you sinister sweetheart!

SIGNORA ARLECCHINO *looks older and wiser.*

There you see, Arlecchino, what a vice virtue is. How can a virtuous woman tempt without temptations? How does she do it, Arlecchino? Study the ways of woman.

He studies them.

Oh! Arlecchino, you're blushing. Don't blush, Arlecchino. What happier thing can a forced virtue become than a practiced bawd? Listen to me, Signora Arlecchino, when you so rust that lovers run from your modest indignation, the time has come to fetch lovers for the lovers. A happy bawd! Fetch and carry lusty maids and lusty men, trip to your grave with love's gold in one hand, love's letters in the other, love's memories in your head and love's trinkets in your pockets, and lie down at last in a paralyzed decorum!

He is seized by the pleasure of his role.

Oh, what a thing it is to be incognito! Everybody, look! Look at the incognito! Who is inside this little darling? Whose memories lie behind these pretty eyes? Whose bosom is swelling behind this swelled bosom? Whose wisdom is behind this folly? Magical Arlecchino, how thoroughly you are tucked away! Nothing can find you out but Cintia and your own salvation. There it is, Arlecchino. Knock, and it will open. Lift your skirts and walk right in! And nothing that has eyes to see can have the wit to stop you. No husbands, no lovers, no old men, no young men——

SCENE 2

FLAMINIA *comes out of her house, and, seeing* ARLECCHINO's *back, says at once.*

FLAMINIA. Arlecchino, have you forgotten about me?

ARLECCHINO. Woman! I have forgotten about you!

FLAMINIA. Cruel Arlecchino, why are you dressed like that? Is this what comes of your promise? Is this how you remember about my husband's teeth?

ARLECCHINO. Your husband's teeth! Little promiser, since I left you, I have been gnashing my own. Arlecchino had neither wine nor meat nor dessert nor what he intended from you, and he has tossed your business from his pocket and is in a hurry pursuing a business of his own.

FLAMINIA. How wrongfully you abuse me, Arlecchino. Could

ACT II, SCENE 2

you not see in my impatience how I longed to be rid of that old crow Coviello and give you that banquet I promised you so fully? Only this favor, only play this one trick on my husband, and see how Flaminia can answer for a promise.

ARLECCHINO. Wise lady, do you think that Arlecchino lives by foolish impulse? Who knows better than Arlecchino the folly of learning the same lesson twice? I will tell you a secret, Flaminia. Once when Arlecchino was rich enough to own a very long sheet of paper, he catalogued on one side all the virtues of wisdom, all the lessons of caution, all the maxims of restraint, and—would you believe it?—they added up to the blessed truth. On the other side, he catalogued all the follies of the world, all sweet promises, all tantalizing hopes, all yearnings and lovely cravings, all the hungers of the body, the soul and the mind, and—do you know?—they added up to heartbreak, anguish, disenchantment and despair. Little promiser, how was a man to choose?

FLAMINIA. Very well, you chose wisdom and so will have nothing to do with me. Then good-by.

ARLECCHINO. No, no, I left wisdom to the wise men, and hugged all the sweet follies to my heart. Wonderful Flaminia, only make your promises tantalizing enough, and you can ask anything of me. Promise me bliss, and tell me what you want me to do.

FLAMINIA. Arlecchino! You dear, clever madman! Hurry into my house and be ready for Pantalone. I have sent for my husband and told him I have found a dentist for him to cure his breath. Hurry into the house, disguise yourself as a dentist, and return. Disappear, Arlecchino, he is coming!

ARLECCHINO. I fly!

FLAMINIA. And remember, not a word of this to Coviello, that awful, jealous man.

ARLECCHINO. Not a word!

He runs into FLAMINIA'S *house.*

SCENE 3

PANTALONE *comes in dragging the chest of lemons.* COVIELLO *and* ZANNI *are superintending his labor and urging him on.*

COVIELLO. This way, Pantalone, shove it this way and pull a little harder! Don't fall, oh, the poor man is falling! His strength——

ZANNI. His strength, keep up his strength, Coviello! He-he-he! Don't fall, Pantalone! Oh, if he falls, the poor man will never get up!

PANTALONE, *aside.* I'll get up, curse you, as you'll never again get up.

COVIELLO. Don't tip the basket, Pantalone!

He screams.

Ah, he's crushing his foot!

ZANNI, *in terror.* His poor old foot! He'll never walk again!

PANTALONE, *aside.* Right through your door, you old eunuch, and walk into your bedroom, and into your bed.

ZANNI. Save his foot!

PANTALONE, *aside.* And keep on walking!

COVIELLO. Thank heaven he didn't stuff it too full of lemons, so that he could still drag it along. You didn't stuff it too full of lemons, did you, Pantalone?

PANTALONE, *as he finally brings the chest to rest.* No, no, there's room enough for a body in it!

ZANNI. Room enough for a body! He-he-he!

COVIELLO. Thank heaven, for your sake, Pantalone. What a burden for a man to drag!

Testing it.

And it's a firm chest, Pantalone? It won't come apart?

PANTALONE. No, no, it could hold a man's weight and not come apart.

ACT II, SCENE 4

ZANNI, *delighted.* A man's weight, oh, a man's weight! He-he-he!

COVIELLO. I'm pleased for your sake, Pantalone. A firm chest and it will not come apart. Aren't you pleased, Zanni, for Pantalone's sake?

ZANNI, *quite obviously.* Delighted, delighted for Pantalone!

COVIELLO, *with ceremony.* Flaminia, my kind neighbor, here is the chest of lemons Pantalone carried for you with the help of his good friend Zanni and myself.

FLAMINIA. A thousand thanks, dear neighbor, and depend upon it, Pantalone will find a way to reward you.

COVIELLO. Generous neighbor! Coviello wants no other reward than the joy of seeing Pantalone foster the delight and comfort of his wife, a good woman, happy to bear her husband many sons, yea, many sons.

PANTALONE. Where is this dentist, Flaminia? Pantalone is ready, girded for his sacrifice.

ZANNI. Girded and trussed! Stuffed, tied, and feathered!

FLAMINIA. Then you are ready, dear husband, for whatever befalls?

ZANNI. Ready? He's ripe and spoiling! Did you ever see a man so ripe for what befalls?

COVIELLO. So be it, honest Flaminia! Let him come.

FLAMINIA, *going to her door and opening it.* Come out, good dentist! My husband is asking for whatever befalls!

SCENE 4

ARLECCHINO *comes out with the air of a high priest emerging from the tabernacle. He wears an immense cloak, a huge hat, and carries a great satchel with instruments.*

ARLECCHINO. *In nomine patris.* Where is the hapless man?

FLAMINIA. Worthy practitioner! Did you find all your comforts while waiting in my house?

ARLECCHINO. *Sanctum sanctorum.* Lead me to my object.

FLAMINIA. Praise heaven and your craft, good man. Here is the willing patient.

ARLECCHINO, *surveying him, raising his hand in blessing.* Simplex simplicimus! Shall we begin?

PANTALONE. Begin.

ARLECCHINO, *drops his satchel to the ground. It falls as though it were laden with bricks.* Bring him a chair!

COVIELLO, *running into* FLAMINIA's *house for it.* A chair, a chair for Pantalone!

ARLECCHINO. A rope!

ZANNI. A rope? He-he, I have just the rope for Pantalone.

And he runs into his house to get it. COVIELLO *deposits the chair in the middle of the stage.*

PANTALONE. A rope? Why do you need a rope?

ARLECCHINO. Be seated, Pantalone.

PANTALONE, *not sitting.* Somebody tell me why he needs a rope.

FLAMINIA. Put your faith in the dentist, Pantalone.

ARLECCHINO *kneels down, pulls open the top of the satchel, and begins the elaborate business of extracting the implements. First, an object resembling a two-foot-long corkscrew. Then, a something that looks like a sledge hammer. He removes an instrument that looks like monstrous calipers. And last, a set of immense pliers, which he holds aloft.*

PANTALONE, *getting ready to run off.* Pantalone, this is your Day of Judgment!

FLAMINIA, *as she,* COVIELLO *and* ZANNI *run to stop him.* Running away? Husband, where is your great courage?

COVIELLO. Stop, Pantalone. What is there to be afraid of?

ZANNI. Is there anyone afraid? Who is afraid? He-he! Not Pantalone!

COVIELLO, *leading* PANTALONE *to the chair, with the help of the others.* No, not Pantalone. Not with his wife beside him. Not with his friends here to give him courage.

PANTALONE, *as he is gently but forcibly seated in the chair.* Tell me why he needs a rope.

ARLECCHINO. Tie him!

PANTALONE *moves to spring out of his chair.*

FLAMINIA, *holding him.* Don't move, Pantalone. For your own sake, dear man, hold your seat!

ZANNI, *dancing and skipping completely around the chair as he winds the rope round and round* PANTALONE *until the patient is completely immobilized.* For your own sake, for your very own sake, dear sweet Pantalone. For your sake, for you, he-he, for nobody else but you!

ARLECCHINO. *In manus tuas!*

Humming, he moves toward PANTALONE'S *mouth, while the others stand absolutely silent and breathless with interest. He moves the pliers toward* PANTALONE'S *mouth, almost sticks his nose into it, then, hurling himself back across the stage away from* PANTALONE'S *offending breath, he shouts at him, waving the pliers to emphasize his wrath.*

Rubrificationibus! Excrementabilis! Fungi! Fungi!

He lunges back into his satchel and produces two long handles which he attaches to the pliers, and, thus keeping his distance, examines the open maw of PANTALONE *from about six feet away. He m'hms and ahas for a while, and pokes about in* PANTALONE'S *mouth with the functional end of the pliers. Suddenly he barks:*

All!

and waves the pliers with a broad gesture, almost knocking PANTALONE'S *teeth out of his mouth at a stroke.* PANTALONE *groans.*

PANTALONE. Learned sir, hunt about for a while and see if there are any you can save.

ARLECCHINO. We shall see. OPEN!

PANTALONE *throws his mouth open, and* ARLECCHINO *again puts the pliers into it.*

Gently, gently——

And when he presumes he has them where he wants them, with a shout he leaps at PANTALONE, *and, standing on the patient's lap, he works them up and down like a man possessed.* PANTALONE *shrieks and groans in agony, tilts his chair backward, and the spectators of his torment, in various conditions of helpfulness and excitement, support the chair, lend a hand to* ARLECCHINO *in working the pliers and shout instructions to* PANTALONE *as follows:*

FLAMINIA. Hold on a little longer, Pantalone!

ZANNI. You're doing well, Pantalone, very well!

COVIELLO. Let it happen, Pantalone! Don't fight it!

At last ARLECCHINO *dismounts with a great white object, dripping blood from its ragged end, trapped in the teeth of the pliers.*

PANTALONE, *hanging limp with exhaustion, lifts his head like a dying man.* Flaminia! Where is he? Has he flown away?

ARLECCHINO, *holding up the pliers like a sword, announces:* ONE!!

PANTALONE, *galvanized into life by this announcement, yells:* No more, no more!

ZANNI. No more?

FLAMINIA. Husband! The good dentist has only just begun!

ARLECCHINO. Open! Open again!

PANTALONE. Not for the Devil himself! Devil! Not for salvation!

ARLECCHINO. *Deus avertat!* Open his mouth!

He bangs the sledge hammer on the ground.

PANTALONE. Never! Never will that fiend see the inside of my mouth again!

FLAMINIA. See it! He will smell it! In the North of England they will smell it! Do you want me to die of the stink of your breath?

PANTALONE, *in a spasm of fury, throws the chair at* ARLECCHINO, *who runs out amid screaming.* If I kill the world with this breath, let that hellhound be the first to go! Let it stink! Let it breathe fire! But it will stay as it is! Stay as it is!

He has been tossing ARLECCHINO's *instruments and satchel after the fleeing* ARLECCHINO, *who runs out to the left, and after* ZANNI *and* COVIELLO, *who run out to the right.* FLAMINIA *takes refuge in her house.*

As they run:

ZANNI. He's mad! Mad!

ACT II, SCENE 5

COVIELLO. Pantalone's gone mad!

FLAMINIA. Help! My husband is possessed!

And they are gone.

SCENE 5

PANTALONE. POSSESSED!! Of what am I possessed? Of a devil wife who brings devils to tear teeth out of my jaws! Of a breath that fells men, would shrink flowers, and make even the canal hold its nose! Oh, my life, what a toothache you've become! Where is that consolation? Find her out, Pantalone, find her and have her! Time or no time, tooth or no tooth, hug your consolation to you now! Franceschina! Franceschina! A beggar is at your door! Your fond Pantalone has come begging!

SCENE 6

FRANCESCHINA *has come out of her house.*

FRANCESCHINA. Sweet Pantalone! What thievish lout has been knocking the teeth out of your mouth?

PANTALONE. No, my own wife charged me to submit to a dentist, a devilish executioner, who has cost me the remains of my beauty.

FRANCESCHINA. Beauty lies deeper in a man than his teeth. What curious discerning woman was ever put off from a man by the loss of a few teeth?

PANTALONE. Iphigenia! Oh, I pray God your understanding doesn't lead to such another remedy.

FRANCESCHINA. Franceschina has a simple remedy for a man's sorrows. Come with Franceschina, and the whole loss will be made up to you!

PANTALONE, *holding back.* First tell me, good woman—what is my breath?

FRANCESCHINA. What is it? It is breath!

PANTALONE. It doesn't offend you?

FRANCESCHINA. No more than my own!

PANTALONE. Oh, my consolation!

FRANCESCHINA. How, Pantalone?

PANTALONE. We are the same odor!

They go into FRANCESCHINA's *house.*

SCENE 7

LEANDRO *comes in disguised as a woman. His disguise is identical with* ARLECCHINO's.

LEANDRO. A clear night, a clear road, a clear disguise—a clear pleasure! Oh, what a man will do to keep a husband smiling! Waste no time on monologues, Leandro. Get into Cintia's house before that other country maiden comes to call.

He knocks at her door.

Cintia! Oh Lord, will she put me to the test of ardor before I get into the house?

CINTIA, *from inside the house*. Who is there? Can it be my little country cousin?

LEANDRO. She will! Well, Leandro, it's a battle of metaphors tonight, right up to the door of the bedroom.

CINTIA, *coming out*. Ah, Leandro! So humbled as to mock his manhood! Cruel Cintia, to humble her lover with a foolish disguise! Oh my darling, be sure, be sure that from this debasement, Cintia will have you rise. She will see to it!

LEANDRO. My tender minister, how could I doubt? Don't I remember how, out of baseness, you have made me rise before?

CINTIA. Memories, Leandro, precious memories. How many memories we have hoarded up, Leandro!

LEANDRO. Of meetings and partings, of fallings and risings——

CINTIA. In the brightness of the moon, remember?
LEANDRO. In the downpour at noon, can I forget?
CINTIA. At Matins, at Lauds, at each of the canonical hours!
LEANDRO. Oh, my breviary, my canon, my office! Oh, my divine service!
CINTIA. My sanctity!
LEANDRO. My holiness, come—let us pray!

He rushes her into the house.

SCENE 8

COVIELLO *and* ZANNI *come in cautiously.*

COVIELLO. Is he gone?
ZANNI. He is gone. Oh, Pantalone! Now you're a mad dog as well as a fool!
COVIELLO. Do you have the keys to the chest?
ZANNI. Yes, from Pantalone's pocket.
COVIELLO, *stops and puzzles over this.* When did you get them?
ZANNI. When the fool was tied in the chair, and howling about losing a tooth.
COVIELLO. But you were not near his pocket!
ZANNI, *opening the chest.* I have them just the same.
COVIELLO. But, Zanni, if you weren't near his pocket, the action isn't probable. It isn't even possible!
ZANNI, *irate.* Is this Aristotle or *commedia*? Get into the chest.
COVIELLO. Curses on these lemons. Can you carry me and all the lemons too?
ZANNI. Yes, yes, get in. Zanni can bear the burden for Pantalone. Have no fear, Coviello. Get in.

COVIELLO gets into the chest. ZANNI *locks the chest and sits on it.*

Oh, let me sit down and enjoy this moment! Oh, Pantalone, you no-father! Here is your offspring in this chest, and here is your deliverer sitting on it. In a moment, in less than a moment, Zanni will undo you, you no-husband!

COVIELLO, *from inside the chest.* What are you waiting for, Zanni? Pick up the chest and carry me into the house.

ZANNI. He-he-he! If you could see me now, Pantalone! Wherever you are, what a pity you can't see me now, you fool, you trusting folly, you no-father and no-husband!

COVIELLO. Hurry and get me inside and go back to your own house before you are missed there. Don't you want to hurry home?

ZANNI. Yes, yes, there is entertainment for me at home too, but this moment is so blessed, I can't bear to give it up for what is waiting for me in my own house. He-he-he! Oh, Pantalone, you old, blind, deaf, mad, trusting fool! Older than the wisest man, and he knows nothing!

COVIELLO. Zanni, what's the matter? Is the chest too heavy for you?

ZANNI. Too heavy for me? He-he! Zanni can bear anything for Pantalone! If only it is for Pantalone, Zanni can bear it. Come, into the house!

He lifts the chest with one hand, and holding it as though it were paper, he trots to FLAMINIA'S *door.* Flaminia, here are your lemons!

FLAMINIA, *opening the door and calling with rapture.* Welcome, welcome, Zanni!

ZANNI *runs into the house with the chest.*

SCENE 9

ARLECCHINO *comes in dressed as a woman again.*

ARLECCHINO. At last, a clear road to Cintia's door! A clear night, a clear disguise—a clear pleasure! Oh, what a man will do to keep a husband smiling! What a lovely conceit, Arlecchino! Where is the lover who, on the brink of his salvation, can conceit you such a conceit? It's a wise head you carry, Arlecchino!

Going to CINTIA's *door.*

Oh, Cintia! Wisdom is here for salvation! Your little cousin is here from the country, just arrived, Cintia, to learn all about the town's good ways.

CINTIA, *from inside the house.* My little country cousin is already in my house! What devil is out there wanting to make a fool of Cintia?

ARLECCHINO. No, Cintia, I am not in your house, I am out here waiting to get in. Open the door and you will see me just as you expected to.

CINTIA, *inside.* Go away and stop your lying. You're not out there, but sitting beside me now, and—oh!

She laughs.

You're tickling me!

ARLECCHINO. Tickling you? I'm not even near you. Open the door and I'll be glad to tickle you.

CINTIA. Stop tickling me!

ARLECCHINO. Not until you let me in. Let me in and I'll stop tickling you gladly, Cintia.

CINTIA, *inside.* Oh, that's better, darling little cousin. Darling, darling little cousin, that's very nice.

ARLECCHINO. What's very nice? Open the door, Cintia, so that I can see what I am doing! Come out here and you'll see me where I say I am. Won't you believe your senses? Won't you believe your eyes?

CINTIA, *poking her head out the door.* My senses much more than my eyes. What a dreadful liar you are! You tell me I can see you there when all the time I can feel you here.

ARLECCHINO. But you *see* me! I am here, Cintia, see? You can't feel me there if you see me here.

CINTIA. Dull man! To feel only what he sees! Well then see what Cintia feels and feel as you please about what you see!

She ushers LEANDRO *into* ARLECCHINO's *sight.*

SCENE 10

ARLECCHINO. Arlecchino! What am I doing there?
He turns around and speaks to the space behind him.
Arlecchino, Arlecchino—are you with me? If you are with me here, then what are you doing there?
He walks closer to LEANDRO *and says to him:*
You, Arlecchino—tell me—which of me are you?

LEANDRO, *in echo.* You, Arlecchino—tell me—which of me are you?

ARLECCHINO, *turning to the invisible* ARLECCHINO. You, Arlecchino—— Where are you?—Oh—tell me——
Whispering to the invisible one.
Did you know about this abbreviated Arlecchino?
Turning to LEANDRO *prayerfully.*
Oh, little ghost of Arlecchino, go away from the door and let me be alone with Cintia!

LEANDRO, *echoing again.* Oh, little ghost of Arlecchino, go away from the door and let me be alone with Cintia!

ARLECCHINO, *pinching himself to demonstrate.* But look at me, ghost, I am not a ghost! I am flesh, flesh, and need no help from you, spirit, to win my salvation! Go away!

LEANDRO, *pinching himself also, and echoing* ARLECCHINO *again.* But look at me, ghost, I am not a ghost! I am flesh, flesh, and need no help from you, spirit, to win my salvation! Go away!
He goes back into the house, after CINTIA.

SCENE 11

ARLECCHINO, *crying after the departed* LEANDRO. Arlecchino! Don't go back alone! Oh my soul, what good is your salvation without my flesh to share in it? Spirit Arlecchino! *Me* Arlecchino! Take this devilish flesh with you!

Turning away from the house in despair.

Oh, Arlecchino, this is the worst trick of all! To have your soul saved without your body! What man can endure such a cheat and disappointment!

He stops suddenly, and says to himself, as though he didn't want to be overheard:

Hey, Arlecchino! Come here! Can you live like a clever liar? No! Then die like an honest man! Throw off your disguises and be yourself!

He begins to tear off his disguise and throws the pieces of it into the audience.

Pick your lying spirit clean, cast out your fraudulent soul, throw away your art, that phantom, toss off that cheat, your laughter. Let your immortal flesh die as naked as the truth.

He is divested of his disguise, and left plain ARLECCHINO.

There you are, Arlecchino—— All right—kill yourself.

He clutches his throat and begins to choke himself.

SCENE 12

ZANNI *comes out of* FLAMINIA's *house.*

ZANNI, *seeing* ARLECCHINO. Doctor! Miraculous doctor! How did you save yourself from Hell?

ARLECCHINO. I was interrupted.

ZANNI. Were you there, great man? Did the Devil carry you all the way to Hell?

ARLECCHINO. To its very door.

ZANNI. What did you see there? Tell me, whom did you meet?

ARLECCHINO. I'll tell you. When I got to the very gate, when I knocked to get in—on the strength of a promise, mind you —the door opened, someone came out to meet me—— And who do you think it was?

ZANNI. Who? Who? A devil?

ARLECCHINO. Worse, much worse!

ZANNI. A monster? A three-headed thing?

ARLECCHINO. Worse than that!

ZANNI. What? What? What horror met you?

ARLECCHINO. Myself! Myself came to the door, told me to go away, and went back in without me!

ZANNI. A miracle. A miracle in Hell. Come, Franceschina must hear about this. Franceschina! Franceschina!

ARLECCHINO. Another time, Zanni. The doctor must get back to some business he was attending to.

ZANNI. No, no. Franceschina must see the good doctor again, and have a magician to tend her child. Come out, Franceschina, the magical doctor is back!

SCENE 13

FRANCESCHINA *comes out with the laundry basket, this time filled with laundry.*

FRANCESCHINA. Why are you interrupting me in the midst of nursing your child?

ZANNI. Forgive me, Franceschina, were you in the midst of nursing him?

FRANCESCHINA. Right in the midst of it, you idiot, when you shouted.

ZANNI. Are you fondling him, Franceschina, are you showing him great love and tenderness?

FRANCESCHINA. More than you could imagine, you fool, greater than you could dream of.

ZANNI. Let me come in and play a bit with the little dear. Do you think, Doctor, he will be happy to see his father?

FRANCESCHINA. Play with him? You mad old folly, what are you thinking of? He will scratch out your eyes.

ZANNI. What? He would scratch out the eyes of his loving father?

FRANCESCHINA. Run to the market stalls and bring him a toy. Come to see him with a toy in your hands, and then you can play with him.

ZANNI. A toy? Where am I to get a toy in the middle of the night?

FRANCESCHINA. Run, you old palsy, and don't come back until you find him a toy.

ZANNI. If I do, will he be happy to see me then?

FRANCESCHINA. He will kiss you and bless you, kiss you and bless you forever.

ZANNI. I'll find him a toy, Franceschina. Keep him happy, good mother, until I return.

FRANCESCHINA, *as* ZANNI *is running out*. He'll be happy until you return, I promise you.

ZANNI *runs out*.

SCENE 14

FRANCESCHINA, *turns furiously on* ARLECCHINO *as soon as* ZANNI *has gone*. Liar. Cheat. You fraud of a doctor. Are you standing there accusing me of breaking my word?

ARLECCHINO. Good woman, I haven't opened my mouth.

FRANCESCHINA. Deceit! Deceit! I swear, Franceschina will be quits with you for this abuse. What are you supposing, you lecherous fraud? That Franceschina promised you her virtue, that she swore she would lie with you?

ARLECCHINO. I am supposing nothing, modest lady, except that I want to be off and that you want me to go.

FRANCESCHINA. Lie with you, you foul beast? Give you Franceschina's virtues, you scheming hypocrite? That's what you supposed I promised?

ARLECCHINO. I supposed you supposed——

FRANCESCHINA. You supposed! You supposed! You supposed I promised and then, you cheat, you supposed I would never redeem my promise. Franceschina, to whom honesty is more than all the other virtues. Very well then, you outrage, if you supposed I would bed you, I will bed you for days and days without number, I'll redeem that promise a hundred times, a thousand times over, that you will know that Franceschina knows how to keep her word, and then she will be quits with your lying deceit forever.

ARLECCHINO, *outraged.* Oh, you woman, you think Arlecchino doesn't remember what promises are made to him. Then listen to Arlecchino, for Arlecchino is going to swear by his sacred flesh and blessed hungers. I will hold you to every letter of your oath, woman. Put me through any trial on my memory or my understanding you can think of, and not one iota of it will I forget, not a word, not a sigh, not a wink, not a movement of your limbs will I remember or repeat of what you did without the most perfectly accurate recollection.

FRANCESCHINA. Then you dare Franceschina! Then listen to Franceschina, man, for she will confess what she has never confessed. My lover Pantalone is with me now, and when the will of heaven wears down his own, he will leave my house and you can come in. Wait in this basket—

ARLECCHINO. Oh, that basket!

FRANCESCHINA. In that basket, until he is gone, and then we will see which of us can manage a powerful promise.

ARLECCHINO. Then you dare Arlecchino! I, who can manage a million promises, promises without number. Very well, we shall see!

He climbs into the basket in a fury while saying this.

FRANCESCHINA. Yes, we shall see. Are you ready?

ARLECCHINO. Ready.

And she stuffs the clothing over him in the basket, and ARLECCHINO *sits inside it at the door of her house, invisible.*

FRANCESCHINA. And none of your shouting and yawping, do you hear? It is night, and my neighbors are tucked away in their beds, snoring and dreaming of modesty and heavenly rewards. Don't wake them, do you hear? Don't let them suppose that Franceschina's house is less virtuous than any of theirs. Whisper to me, do you understand?

ARLECCHINO, *whispering from inside the basket.* I understand.

FRANCESCHINA. Then when Pantalone finds it in his weakness to leave, you will enter. Sh! If you value my virtue, not a sound!

She goes in.

SCENE 15

A musician crosses the empty stage, playing and singing. The song to follow Act IV of The Mandrake *might be used.*

SCENE 16

When he is gone PANTALONE *comes out of* FRANCESCHINA'S *house. He yawns and stretches.* LEANDRO *comes out of* CINTIA'S *house and does the same thing. They see each other and start.*

LEANDRO. Pantalone! I thought I was meeting Coviello.

PANTALONE. Leandro! Coming from Coviello's house at this hour!

LEANDRO. And from whose house is Pantalone coming at this hour? Surely not Zanni's, eh, Pantalone?

PANTALONE. We lovers can abide each other's confidence. It was Zanni's house, to be sure. Zanni is such a blind fool, Leandro. What a comfort it is to have such a friend as Zanni!

LEANDRO. As comfortable as having such a friend as Coviello. Quickly, come down the street with me and help me get rid of my masquerade.

PANTALONE. Yes, yes. Then we can come back and masquerade as innocent friends.

LEANDRO. Leandro and Pantalone. Away all night on important business.

PANTALONE. Spoken like a lover.

They go off together.

SCENE 17

ARLECCHINO *sticks his head out of the basket, with the linen draped around him.*

ARLECCHINO. What a fool that vinegar husband is to mix with that oily lover. And what a fool that lover is to let a husband look over his shoulder. Arlecchino, you are wise to stay in the basket in the morning when all the husbands are popping about. Get down, Arlecchino, here come two more wise men.

SCENE 18

COVIELLO *comes out of* PANTALONE'S *house as* ZANNI *comes in with toys.*

COVIELLO. Zanni, what are you carrying?

ZANNI. Ah, Coviello, advise me. Will the little darling like to play with these? Franceschina forbade me to come back without them, and all night long Zanni has run about getting them. Will they make him happy, Coviello? Will they please him?

COVIELLO. How did you come by a child, Zanni? Has someone left one at your door?

ZANNI. That is my secret. Mine and the crafty doctor's who is tending him. And Pantalone will never laugh at me again.

COVIELLO. But we will laugh at him, eh, Zanni? We have both outwitted him. Think, Zanni, that a man lives who is such a fool!

ZANNI. Ah, the world is not wise, Coviello, the world is not wise.

SCENE 19

PANTALONE *and* LEANDRO *come in.*

PANTALONE. Zanni! You have just returned?

LEANDRO. Coviello! How fortunate to meet you now.

COVIELLO. My good friend Leandro!

ZANNI. Pantalone, my dear.

PANTALONE. What are you carrying there, Zanni?

ZANNI. Toys. For my newly arrived child, Pantalone.

PANTALONE. A child! Where is it, Zanni?

ZANNI. With his mother, who has been watching over him this past night.

PANTALONE. Oh, blessed child!

ZANNI. Are you to be blessed too, Pantalone?

PANTALONE. Not so blessed as you, Zanni. Could I be honest, and hope to be blessed in my child as you are in yours?

ZANNI. True, Pantalone, very true.

PANTALONE. Very true, very true.

COVIELLO, *to* PANTALONE. And you have had a good night too, Pantalone?

PANTALONE. Oh, very good, Coviello.

COVIELLO. Untroubled, content?

PANTALONE. As untroubled as Zanni's, good friend.

LEANDRO. But Zanni has been busy all night chasing another's pleasure.

PANTALONE. Pantalone too, my friend.

LEANDRO. Zanni has found pleasure in his charity, and the toys he has there for his loved one.

PANTALONE. Pantalone too, my friend, Pantalone too, as you know better than any man.

ZANNI. And have you found pleasure in charity too, Leandro?

LEANDRO. Oh, great charity. And from a kind of toy, too. And Coviello, the good man, he has shown charity too tonight, don't you think so, Pantalone?

COVIELLO. Charity with toys, Leandro. My whole night has been nothing but charity and toys.

PANTALONE. Charity indeed, Coviello. Great charity.

ZANNI. Well, it was a blessed night indeed, of which all of us have nothing to remember but charity and mercy, and nothing to reap in the morning but gratitude and contentment.

COVIELLO. Yes, a blessed morning.

PANTALONE. A blessed morning, a good morning.

SCENE 20

FLAMINIA *comes out of her house.*

FLAMINIA. Pantalone! Husband! At last you are with me again.

PANTALONE. My own wife, did you miss me?

FLAMINIA. Not once did I shut my eyes for remembering you were gone.

PANTALONE. Dear Flaminia.

CINTIA *comes out of her house.*

CINTIA. Husband! Coviello! Thank God you are back this morning.

COVIELLO. My own Cintia, were you anxious about my being gone?

CINTIA. All night I lay awake wondering when you would return.

COVIELLO. My own Cintia.

FRANCESCHINA *comes out of her house.*

FRANCESCHINA. Zanni, my husband! At last you are back from your errand.

ZANNI. Safe and sound, good Franceschina. Are you happy I did not despair and come back without the toys?

FRANCESCHINA. If you had given up and come back without them, your Franceschina would have been lost.

ZANNI. Excellent mother!

FLAMINIA. A celebration! Dear neighbors, this is a morning for rejoicing. Pantalone and Flaminia ask you all to dine and we will celebrate these happy reunions of true wives and contented husbands.

SEVERALLY. A banquet. Come. Oh, blessed morning—a banquet.

FRANCESCHINA. Zanni, dear husband, bring my laundry basket into the house before we settle to this banquet.

ZANNI. Yes, dear mother, yes, yes.

PANTALONE. Let us help you, Zanni. Coviello, let us help Zanni carry his burden.

ZANNI. Ah, Zanni needs no help with baskets, Pantalone. Zanni can carry baskets.

COVIELLO. For your sake, Zanni.

PANTALONE. For Zanni's sake. All together—

COVIELLO. All together—

ZANNI. All together, friends—heave ho!

Since they have all grasped the basket at the same end, it overturns as they lift it and ARLECCHINO *falls out onto the ground. Consternation.*

COVIELLO. My friend!

PANTALONE. The beggar!

ZANNI. The doctor!

FLAMINIA. My little helper!

CINTIA. My conspirator!

FRANCESCHINA. My promise!

ZANNI. Doctor! What are you doing in my basket?

PANTALONE. Is this the bundle to be carried into your house? What a kindness we were doing for your wife!

ZANNI. Kindness for my wife? Then it was a kindness returned, because only last night I carried a chest into your house, with just such a burden inside it.

COVIELLO. Zanni, don't let the world know that our good friend has a lover coming to his house.

PANTALONE. No, and Pantalone will keep it secret that only this morning did he meet a lover coming out of Coviello's house, who is, as all the world knows, a cuckold!

COVIELLO. Ha! Then tell it he is a lover too, and of Pantalone's wife, whom Pantalone could not please!

PANTALONE. Not please? I, who am a lover and a father too, not please! This from an old jealous cuckold and an impotent old fool!

ZANNI. I impotent! Pantalone calls me impotent! I, who produced a child bigger than Pantalone's! No, no, he did not even produce a child. He produced a chest of lemons. Nothing but a chest of lemons! Ask this devilish doctor what a child I produced yesterday.

PANTALONE. Doctor! That is Coviello's mad country cousin, who cannot utter a syllable out of his mouth.

ZANNI. Latin! Latin comes out of his mouth. And children out of the ground! That is how mad he is.

Running to ARLECCHINO.

Shout Latin at him, shout it and sing it, that he will know you are a man of the science. Tell him in Latin how Zanni gave birth to a child!

PANTALONE. Save your Latin and I will tell you in your mother tongue. If Zanni has a child it is Pantalone's, for Pantalone has lain with his wife and shown her how children are begotten, and how he begot them on the sworn oath of his own wife. Not as old dead fools and cuckolds beget them in their sick fancies!

COVIELLO. Listen to this sick fancy then, and tell Coviello how better to beget a child for Pantalone than by bringing me into his house in a chest of lemons so that I might do what the both of you have lost the memory of, to please a wife and beget a child!

ZANNI. The both of us! A cuckold talks about the both of us! A cuckold tells us how to please a wife!

ACT II, SCENE 20

PANTALONE. Tell us, tell us how to call Leandro to our beds and please our wives. Cuckold!

COVIELLO. I a cuckold!

Pointing to the both of them.

There are cuckolds! Cuckolds! Cuckolds!

PANTALONE *and* ZANNI *also point to both the other old men and all three, jumping about in a circle and pointing at the other two, shout in a blue fury at the others.*

PANTALONE, ZANNI, COVIELLO. Cuckolds! Cuckolds! Cuckolds!

FRANCESCHINA *screams with rage and stops the dance of the cuckolds dead.*

FRANCESCHINA, *when there is silence.* Who are these men to besmirch our virtues? Pantalone! What have you confessed?

FLAMINIA. Coviello! Has your wife deserved this indignity?

CINTIA. Leandro! What has the world learned of our love?

LEANDRO, *coming to the middle of the stage and addressing them all.* What it would have learned without my word, or your reassurance. What it would learn of all these husbands and wives, for now the cat is out of the bag. And what have you lost now that it has learned all? Honest wives, be honest, and just husbands, be fair, do any of you find yourselves this morning bereft of what you had last night? The lovers did not steal and the wives did not lose their virtue in a single night. Virtue sets off meekly in the eye, in the leg, in the beckoning finger, in the slip of the tongue long before she gallops away in the bed. And the eye, the leg, the finger and the tongue are not born bawdy, but learn to wander after the example of the husband or the lesson of the wife. Pantalone, teach your wife modesty, and she will teach you the seemliness of love. Coviello, teach your wife contentment, and she will show you the abandon of love. Zanni— Zanni. Give your wife patience and pray for a heavenly reward. With all this done, you will have wisdom for your folly, and remember this night always as a blessing in disguise.

ARLECCHINO, *approaches* LEANDRO *and pulls his sleeve.* Wise man, can you teach me how I too can find a blessing in this night's disguise? What am I to do to lose my folly and be content with my lot?

LEANDRO, *pointing to the audience*. Do as these good people here are doing. Find wisdom and contentment in a folly greater than your own. Go to the *commedia*, and laugh at Arlecchino.

ARLECCHINO. Wise man, I am Arlecchino, and I have laughed at him until I have cried. Now I am lost, doubly damned, and triply desperate. Thank you for your counsel, wise man. Do you take a fee?

FLAMINIA, *addressing everybody*. Friends, good neighbors, with the help of the basket and the wise Leandro, this morning has been blessed twice over. Come. Into our house, and we can celebrate a contentment that no husbands and wives before us, and on my honor none that will follow us, can ever know on earth. Look at us. Leandro, come, look at your work. Three husbands and three wives, all smiling, and not a single one with a deceit inside him he can call his own. Miraculous lover who makes husbands happy as well as wives, come in and sit beside me, and tell me the secret of turning plain honesty to so much profit. Good neighbors, come.

LEANDRO *goes into* PANTALONE's *house*. FLAMINIA *offers her hand to* PANTALONE.

Husband!

PANTALONE. Dear wife!

They go in hand in hand.

CINTIA. Coviello!

COVIELLO. Dearest Cintia!

They go in hand in hand.

FRANCESCHINA. Zanni!

ZANNI. Ah, well!

They go hand in hand. ARLECCHINO *stands before the door alone for a moment.* FLAMINIA *comes out as he begins to depart.*

SCENE 21

FLAMINIA. Arlecchino, have we forgotten you? Come in, dear fool, and share in our banquet.

ARLECCHINO. Thank you, kind lady, but not for Arlecchino.

FLAMINIA. But, dear Arlecchino, here is a promise without tricks, without buts, without anything that can come of it but a true harvest.

ARLECCHINO. Dearest of all promises, Arlecchino can share no food and drink with you. What would become of Arlecchino with so much meat and wine inside him? Arlecchino has many follies, dear lady, but he is not so foolish as to digest his injuries and drown his wit.

FLAMINIA. But what better thing can you do, fool, than fill your empty stomach and put your folly to sleep?

ARLECCHINO. I can leave them alone, Flaminia. From my empty stomach I get my whole wisdom, and from my folly, my whole prosperity. Besides, dear lady, Arlecchino is in a great hurry to be off to Bergamo.

FLAMINIA. What is in Bergamo?

ARLECCHINO. Oh, there is a certain Isabella, who has a rich husband and a full larder, and—do you know?—Isabella keeps his keys. If I get there before nightfall, she will open the door for me, and Arlecchino will win her and his salvation and everything with his love.

FLAMINIA. Then Flaminia is not so unkind that she will spoil your happiness with meat and wine. Good-by, fool.

ARLECCHINO. Wise and beautiful lady, good-by.

FLAMINIA *goes in.*

SCENE 22

ARLECCHINO. Move, Arlecchino! Oh, you scrawny little centipede, look at him move! Hurry up, Arlecchino. Bergamo by nightfall! Run, run, to Bergamo and your own salvation! *He leaps out.*

CLASSIC DRAMA
From Applause

MARY STUART — FRIEDRICH SCHILLER

Like Mary Stuart herself and the legends which pursued her to her death, Schiller's drama continues to captivate the modern imagination nearly two centuries later. Eric Bentley's lean forceful rendering of the German masterpiece will command the attention of theatre audiences for many years to come.

96 PAGES, 5½ X 8¼
ISBN: 0-936839-00-7
(PAPER) $5.95

Adapted by Eric Bentley
Translated by Joseph Mellish

PHEDRA — JEAN RACINE

Racine's tragedy of a woman trapped in the web of a terrible diseased passion, unspeakable and irresistible, and the vehement contagion that spreads throughout her world.

Glenda Jackson currently stars in the highly acclaimed new stage version by Robert David MacDonald, slated for Broadway this Spring.

72 PAGES, 4½ X 7¼
ISBN: 0-87910-261-6
(PAPER) $6.95

translated by Robert David MacDonald

CELESTINA — FERNANDO DE ROJAS

The central and pervasive situation is a simple one: a dirty old woman is helping a courtly young gentleman to seduce a girl. The wonder of the thing lies in the art with which Fernando de Rojas derives, from such commonplace materials, a towering tragedy—or rather tragi-comedy.

112 PAGES, 5½ X 8¼
ISBN: 0-936839-01-5
(PAPER) $5.95

Adapted by Eric Bentley
Translated by James Mabbe

TOUR DE FARCE
A New Series of
Farce Through the Ages

THE PREGNANT PAUSE or LOVE'S LABOR LOST
by Georges Feydeau
translated by Norman R. Shapiro

Hector Ennepèque, first-time father-to-be, is in extended labor and protracted comic convulsions over his wife Léonie's imminent delivery. Before the baby's arrival, this hilarious farce gives birth to multiple comic harangues all aimed at the helpless henpecked husband. When Hector tries to rebound from the recriminations of his aristocratic in-laws, he is swatted aside by an Amazon midwife who takes charge of everything.

A brilliant tableau of conjugal chaos by the master of the genre.

Cast: two males, four females. One set, interior
$5.95 (paper) 96 pages, 5½ x 8¼
ISBN: 0-936839-58-9

THE BRAZILIAN
by Henri Meilhac and Ludovic Halévy
translated by Norman R. Shapiro

Two amorous actresses are out to capture the affections of a wealthy Paris producer. The wily Micheline spreads the rumor that Rafaella is being courted by a murderously jealous Brazilian. But her plot backfires when, instead of cooling his passions down, the producer's interest heats up. Micheline is non-plussed when the tempestuous Brazilian suitor actually shows up at Rafaella's house. The mad improvisation which follows is a romp in the best tradition of door-slamming French bedroom farce.

Cast: two males, three females. One set, interior
$5.95 (paper) 96 pages, 5 x 7
ISBN: 0-936839-59-7

SEEDS OF MODERN DRAMA

Introduced and Edited by Norris Houghton

THERESE RAQUIN
ZOLA

AN ENEMY OF THE PEOPLE
IBSEN

MISS JULIE
STRINDBERG

THE WEAVERS
HAUPTMANN

THE SEA GULL
CHEKHOV

Five great forces · Chekhov, Hauptmann, Ibsen, Strindberg and Zola dramatists whose work define, embrace and transcend the trends and genres of the modern stage, meet here in this extraordinary exhibition of their sustained and sustaining power in today's theatre.

The ideal text for any course venturing into modern drama, Norris Houghton's volume boasts five landmark plays in distinguished modern translations.

ISBN: 0-936839-15-5 PAPER: $9.95
448 pages, 5½ x 8¼

ORDER FOR FALL CLASSES TODAY!

"FIVE SPLENDID PLAYS... ENJOYABLE TO READ AND AS TIMELY TO PRODUCE.*"

**Plays by American Women
Edited and with an introduction
by Judith E. Barlow**

*"Barlow's introduction not only offers a description and analysis of the five playwrights but also sets them in an historical context."

—Booklist

A MAN'S WORLD
by Rachel Crothers
TRIFLES
by Susan Glaspell
MISS LULU BETT
by Zona Gale
PLUMES
by Georgia Douglas Johnson
MACHINAL
by Sophie Treadwell

These important dramatists did more than write significant new plays; they introduced to the American stage a new and vital character; the modern American woman in her quest for a forceful role in a changing American scene. It will be hard to remember that these women playwrights were ever forgotten.

The Brute and Other Farces
by Anton Chekhov
Edited by Eric Bentley

"INDISPENSABLE!"
—*Robert Brustein*
Director, Loeb Drama
Center
Harvard University

The blustering, stuttering eloquence of Chekhov's unlikely heroes has endured to shape the voice of contemporary theatre. This volume presents seven minor masterpieces:

HARMFULNESS OF TOBACCO

SWAN SONG

MARRIAGE PROPOSAL

THE CELEBRATION

A WEDDING

SUMMER IN THE COUNTRY

THE BRUTE

128 pages, 5½ × 8¼
(paper) $5.95
(cloth) $14.95

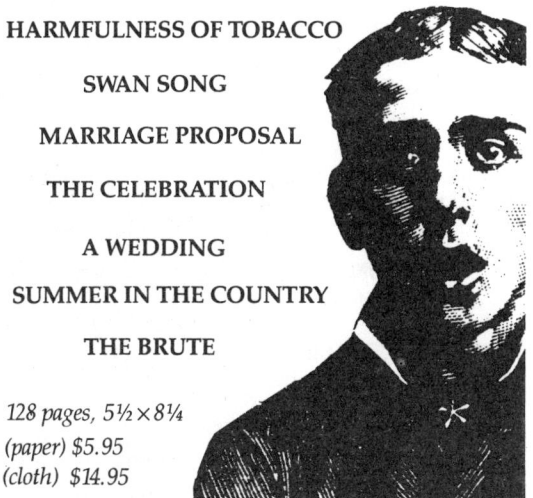

Nineteenth-Century American Plays
Edited by Myron Matlaw

"BRAVO! ESSENTIAL
FOR ALL THOSE
INTERESTED IN
AMERICAN THEATRE."
—*Brooks McNamara*
Director
The Shubert Archive

From Broadway to Topeka these four smash hits were the staples of the American dramatic repertoire. Their revival in this landmark collection will once again bring America to its feet!

MARGARET FLEMING
James A. Herne

THE OCTOROON
Dion Boucicault

FASHION
Anna Cora Mowatt

RIP van WINKLE
Joseph Jefferson

272 pages, 5½ × 8¼
(paper) $8.95
(cloth) $18.95

ERIC BENTLEY'S
Once Again The Editor of
THE MODERN THEATRE Assembles The

THE MISANTHROPE and other French Classics
Edited by Eric Bentley

THE MISANTHROPE Moliere
English Version by Richard Wilbur

PHAEDRA Racine
English Version by Robert Lowell

THE CID Corneille
English Version by James Schevill

FIGARO'S MARRIAGE Beaumarchais
English Version by Jacques Barzun

ISBN: 0-936839-19-8
(paper) $7.95
320 pages, 5½ x 8¼, Notes

LIFE IS A DREAM and Other Spanish Classics Edited by Eric Bentley. Translated by Roy Campbell

LIFE IS A DREAM by Calderon de la Barca

FUENTE OVEJUNA by Lope de Vega

THE TRICKSTER OF SEVILLE by Tirso de Molina

THE SIEGE OF NUMANTIA by Miguel de Cervantes

ISBN:0-87910-244-6 (paper) $8.95 (cloth) $18.95
304 pages, 5½ x 8¼, Notes

DRAMATIC REPERTOIRE
THE CLASSIC THEATRE And
World's Great Drama For the American Stage.

THE SERVANT OF TWO MASTERS and Other Italian Classics
Edited by Eric Bentley

THE SERVANT OF TWO MASTERS Goldoni
English Version by Edward Dent

THE KING STAG Gozzi
English Version by Carl Wildman

THE MANDRAKE Machiavelli
English Version by Frederick May and Eric Bentley

RUZZANTE RETURNS FROM THE WARS Beolco
English Version by Angela Ingold and Theodore Hoffman

ISBN: 0-936839-20-1
(paper) $7.95
272 pages, 5½ x 8¼, Notes

BEFORE BRECHT: Four German Plays
Edited and Translated by Eric Bentley

LEONCE AND LENA by Georg Buchner

LA RONDE by Arthur Schnitzler

SPRING AWAKENING by Frank Wedekind

UNDERPANTS by Carl Sternheim

ISBN: 0-87910-229-2 (paper) $8.95 (cloth) $18.95
272 pages, 5½ x 8¼, Notes

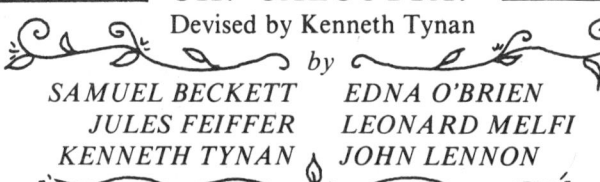

OH! CALCUTTA!
Devised by Kenneth Tynan

by

*SAMUEL BECKETT   EDNA O'BRIEN
JULES FEIFFER   LEONARD MELFI
KENNETH TYNAN   JOHN LENNON*

In *Oh! Calcutta!* Mr. Tynan has assembled a group of sketches which deal with almost every conceivable erotic fantasy and sexual reality that Western man has dreamt up or experienced. The distinguished roster of authors includes Samuel Beckett, Edna O'Brien, Jules Feiffer, Leonard Melfi, John Lennon, and, not to be outdone, Kenneth Tynan himself.

The title of this revue, which is taken from the title of a painting by the French Surrealist painter Clovis Trouille, contains a phonetic French pun: "Oh! Quelle — — — t'as!" Or, freely translated: "Oh! What a lovely — — — you have!"

$5.95 (paper)
ISBN: 0-936839-48-1

LONDON'S BEST PLAYS FROM APPLAUSE

THE SHELTER
BY CARYL PHILLIPS

"Phillips reaches beyond the 'black theatre' ghetto."
—Sunday Times

"More anguished than angry, with some wit and much feeling, Phillips drives his point home."
—Time Out

$7.95 (paper)

UP 'N' UNDER
BY JOHN GODBER

**WINNER OF THE LAURENCE OLIVIER AWARD
for Comedy of the Year**

Godber's smash West End hit follows the outrageous fortunes of the Wheatsheaf Arms amateur rugby side in their battle to defeat their arch rivals, the mean men of the Cobblers Arms

$7.95 (paper)

Philistines by Maxim Gorky

PHILISTINES, Gorky's first play, was given a brilliant new life in Hughes' translation, performed by the Royal Shakespear Company.

English Version by Dusty Hughes

$8.95 (paper)

The Seagull by Anton Chekhov

"The play has been flooded with light, like a room with the curtains drawn back."
—Sunday Times

"A sparkling new translation...suffused with pathos and humour."
—Oxford Times

Translated by Tania Alexander and Charles Sturridge

$7.95 (paper)